The Essential Foodie

ELEVATE YOUR KITCHEN
WITH ESSENTIAL OILS

The Essential Foodie

ELEVATE YOUR KITCHEN
WITH ESSENTIAL OILS

JULEZ WEINBERG

Cultivate Wellness, LLC
Published by Oil Life

The Drop Down information for the blends is courtesy of doterra.com.

For more information on any of these subjects, please visit doterra.com.

Library of Congress Cataloguing-in-Publication data
978-1-7923-4704-7

DISCLAIMER
This book has been created with the intention to provide information to help educate the reader in regard to the subject matter covered. It is sold with the understanding that the author is not liable for the misconception, misunderstanding, and misuse of any of the information provided. The information in this book is not provided with the intention to diagnose, prescribe, or treat any disease, illness, or injured condition of the body. The author of this book shall have neither liability or responsibility to any person or entity with respect to any loss, damage, or injury caused, or allegedly to be caused, directly or indirectly by the information contained within this book. The information provided in this book is in no way intended as a substitute for professional medical counseling. Anyone suffering from any disease, illness, or injury should consult a qualified health professional.

Creative Director: Quinn Curtis

Photography: Caressa Frietz

Design: Katrina Sutton

DEDICATION

While the concept for this book was created long ago, the bulk of it was written during the pandemic of 2020. I dedicate this book to my entire human family. These are transformative times for all of us. May we be blessed with the strength to choose what is right and true, the wisdom to know the difference, and the ability to recognize we are *one*.

Gratitude

I will first express my deepest gratitude to whom many refer to as God, and whom others call the All Mighty Presence, Great Spirit, Divine Mother, Divine Father, Buddha, Krishna, Jesus, Mary, Allah, or Yahweh: There are so many other wonderful ways we address the All That Is. Thank you for your eternal presence in my life. Thank you for helping me to be a vessel of creative expression, love, and beauty in the world. I am ever so grateful to you and humbled by you.

I begin my journey of gratitude with my love, my dearest friend, my amazing business partner and precious spouse, Meredith Kelly. I am the luckiest girl on the planet to be supported by you in this life. Thank you for always encouraging me to share my gifts with the world. Thank you for being a constant source of inspiration. Thank you for being the number one taste-tester for all of my crazy concoctions. Thank you for always believing in me, even when I had lost my way and didn't believe in myself. Thank you for being the one to gently guide me back into the world of aromatic plants and the gift of essential oils. Thank you for being my muse. I love you with all my heart and feel excited and inspired to continue creating with you in this lifetime.

I would like to express my deep gratitude to the founding executives at dōTERRA®—Emily Wright, Dave Sterling, Dr. David Hill, Corey Lindley, Rob Young, Gregory Cook, and Mark Wolfert—for creating a company with the integrity and standards which allow for complete and total freedom to bring these essential oil–infused recipes to life. Because of your dedication and commitment to quality, the world gets to experience these gifts of the earth every day, and I am completely grateful to each of you for this. Thank you.

To Marnie Harrison, I am utterly grateful to you for introducing us to dōTERRA. Thank you for your patience and support. You brought us both something that has changed our lives forever.

I would like to thank the farmers who grow these beautiful aromatic plants, and all of the people who are involved, from seed to bottle. It takes a lot of time and dedication to create an essential oil. Thank you for your hard work and commitment to making sure we get the best essential oils on the planet. I am truly grateful for all that you do to ensure this process and the end results.

I would like to thank our dōTERRA team, Team Cultivate Wellness. You all amaze me each and every day with your passion for sharing these beautiful oils with the world. Your support and love for *The Essential Mixologist* body of work has been a joy and a blessing. I love receiving texts from so many of you asking for different recipes, and I am excited for this new body of work and how it will impact your journeys. I am grateful for each and every one of you. I hope you will all enjoy this book as much as my first one.

I would like to thank my many friends (too many to mention) and family for always encouraging my creations and for enjoying them each time I have had the honor of cooking something special for you. You know who you are; we have shared a meal or two, and I'm always grateful for our time together.

To my mother, Sheila, thank you for sharing your love for creating things in the kitchen with me at an early age and for always believing in me. I love you.

To my sister, Barri, thank you for always believing in me and for thinking of ways to help me share my message with the world. I love you.

To my mother-in-law, Cyndi, thank you for encouraging me over the years to put out a recipe book. I finally followed your gentle guidance, and now we are on number two. I love you.

To Kerri Ialongo-Gillette, thank you for recognizing the plant medicine woman and alchemist living within me and for inviting me to open Herbalicious with you. It changed my life in so many ways, fortified my connection to the plant kingdom, and created a place for the love of my life to find me. I am so totally grateful for your presence in my life.

To Jason Plant at Oil Life, thank you for taking a chance on my first book and for believing in my ideas enough to partner with me on the second one. I am grateful for your openness and willingness to be different, and most of all, for your kindness and your friendship.

To Quinn Curtis, thank you for being as passionate about this book as I am. You have been a true ally and extension of me through the entire post-writing production process. I am truly grateful for all the time and energy you gave to this project. It has been a beautiful journey working with you.

To Emily Smith, thank you for being a delightful addition to this book. Having someone who scrutinizes things in the same compulsive way I do has been music to my soul. I am grateful for your keen eye as an editor and for your talent to wordsmith your way into my brain.

To Caressa Frietz, thank you for being the photographer I could not be for this project. Letting go was challenging, but having you on the other side of the lens was worth it.

To Katrina Sutton, thank you for all of the time and effort you gave to the impeccable layout and design of this book. I am grateful for all of your time and energy. It looks amazing!

To Melanie Clark, thank you for turning my culinary ideas into culinary masterpieces—I was told everything on the shoot tasted fabulous!

To Brooke Woolf, thank you for sprinkling your magical aesthetic dust on everything—the composition of each dish in the photos are beautiful.

Lastly, I would like to directly thank the aromatic plants and the essential oils themselves. You are all like dear friends with distinct personalities, properties, and, of course, signature aromas. I know you are a living, breathing life force on this planet, and the world needs you now more than ever. I am in complete awe of your magic and in total gratitude for your presence on the earth and in my life. Thank you, thank you, thank you.

Salutations

I've said it before, and I'll say it again. I've always considered myself a purist at heart: I love items that are homegrown and made from scratch. I appreciate the process of things, especially when it comes to food and drink. My palate doesn't like to be overstimulated by synthetic and contrived flavors or lackluster processed ingredients. I'm interested in the taste of real fruits, vegetables, plants, flowers, roots, and herbs. I believe many of us have lost our awareness of these magical ingredients, and in our poor attempt to create a replacement for what nature has already provided, we have created a synthetic cacophony of toxicity.

My philosophy is not unique. I'm part of a growing movement that encourages the use of ingredients in their purest forms and the craft creation of as much of what we put into our bodies as is possible. I'm a farm-to-table, pier-to-plate, locavore, slow food, organic, non-GMO, artisan, curated, craft cocktail kind of girl. There, I said it. Now, let's talk about what this book is really about.

The Essential Foodie is about the art of maximizing flavor and weaving medicinal ingredients into food through essential oils. I'm not a renowned chef (yet), and this book is not about me waving around my titles or credentials. I'm just a girl who loves to create with nature. Throughout my journey, I have cultivated a bible of recipes that have captivated the palates of hundreds of people—enough to finally encourage me to write a cookbook and share it with the world.

I encourage you to get familiar with the information I provide about each of the essential oils being used in these recipes. Each time you create or eat these recipes, you are opening yourself up to a world of flavor, an aromatic feast of the senses, and most importantly, an array of beautiful, natural solutions from the plant kingdom to support your body, mind, and spirit.

The Essential Foodie is an invitation to your inner alchemist—an invitation to play and to create the most amazing dishes with health-enhancing properties from the comfort of your home. It's a book about embracing the ease of using essential oils in your kitchen and the simplicity of sharing not just a meal with friends, but a medicinal meal with friends.

ENJOY THE JOURNEY ... BON APPÉTIT!

Always with love, Julez

CONTENTS

Savory Soups

Finishing with Aromatic Integration

Libations from *The Essential Mixologist*

Conclusion

AN ALCHEMIST IS *Born*

If you happened to read my first book, *The Essential Mixologist*, thank you! You're probably already familiar with how I came to love essential oils. In the spirit of saying hello for the first time to all my new readers, I'd like to share my journey on becoming an essential oils foodie.

I'm a tree hugger, and I recognized the symbiotic relationship between plants and humans at a very early age. Plants make oxygen, an important role in sustaining our life force. Plants also create food for us to eat; medicine that can heal our bodies, minds, and spirits; various other useful commodities; and beauty all around us in the form of vivid colors. Some plants—the aromatic plant kingdom specifically—create essential oils, which are the focus of this book. Although I appreciated plants early on, an unconventional experience later in my life further cemented my relationship with them.

When I was in my early-to-mid-twenties, I was visiting friends in New Jersey. It was a beautiful late summer day, and I was lying in a hammock in the backyard. Everything was so alive: I could smell the fragrances of many different flowers, herbs, and trees as a slight breeze blew. In the distance, I heard laughter on the wind. It was so sweet and genuine that I began to laugh with it. As I laughed with the wind, a thought filled my mind. I heard, "Pay attention to us. We will be paying your bills." I was instantly aware that it was a message from the plants. It sounds kooky, but it happened. I started laughing even louder. At that point, my friends yelled over and asked if everything was okay. I quickly pulled myself together and said I was fine and that I had thought of a funny memory.

I laid back in that hammock for quite some time. I could feel the energy of the forest with all of its beauty pulsating around me. It was magical.

I had no idea what it meant in the moment, but several months later, I was studying herbs. I had become co-owner of Herbalicious, a health and wellness business where we provided herbal consultations along with other services and sold herbal plant medicine in all forms.

At Herbalicious I met essential oils for the first time. It was truly love at first smell. I fell in love so deeply that at times I was brought to tears by my experiences with the essential oils. My connection with this wonderful and magical world of aromatic plants was strong; it was like meeting old friends again. I immediately began channeling an inner alchemist who felt as though she had been lying dormant in me. Discovering this part of myself, I was at home with my soul.

I soon attracted a teacher—a fellow alchemist. He taught me many things about blending essential oils and using them in a variety of ways to assist the body, mind, and spirit. It was something I felt like I already intuitively understood, and my ability to create potions for myself and for others quickly moved into action and expression. I even created a blending station in the cellar of Herbalicious. It was my own space to create magic and connect with the plants, and I learned a lot about them during that time.

I traveled to Florida one weekend to meet my teacher and friends and learn more about essential oils. When we came to the end of our day, I suggested we break for cocktails. I was a bartender throughout college and for years after: I liked the

fun of it, and the extra cash. I had always enjoyed making drinks using unique ingredients. My teacher had brought a special jasmine essential oil from a pure source, and I had fallen in love with the aroma and the energy of that plant. I asked if it would be okay for me to use a little to create a round of cocktails for us, and he agreed wholeheartedly that this would be a wonderful experiment.

This was the birthing moment where my alchemy was taken to a whole new level of expression, and my first aromatic cocktail was born: a jasmine spritzer. It was divine. We all felt like we were drinking the nectar of the Gods. It was beautiful and aromatic, and its effects on the psyche were amazing—we all felt relaxed and totally calm.

I began experimenting with high-grade essential oils I knew were from trusted sources. Over time, I created many recipes of unique essential oil–infused cocktails that became well-known where I lived. I started receiving invitations to experiment with these concoctions at parties, and I became known as a mixologist and alchemist.

However, life took me away from Herbalicious and back to my original career choice as a producer, and my sweetheart and I moved to the West Coast. I stayed connected to the essential oils; it seemed they followed me wherever I went. When I say they were always around me, I mean they were always around me. I used them personally and continued to share them. They remained a constant in my life, like trusted friends that were there when I needed them.

Several years later, life brought me full circle once again. My career as a producer reached an exciting high point and then suddenly imploded. Let's say it had everything to do with the economy crashing and all investment capital coming to a screeching halt. Like so many others at that time, I found myself at a crossroads without any advance warning.

I wound up moving back to the East Coast. Shortly after the move, a friend sent me a care package of essential oils from a company called dōTERRA®. When I opened a bottle, I immediately knew that these oils were very different from others I had used. At that point, I was familiar with quality and had been collecting the best essential oils I could find for many years. These oils were on another level. They smelled crisper and they worked faster—they were superior in all ways. I was astounded by the quality. I began using them exactly as I had been using essential oils for many years, and the results I got were better—they worked every time.

I started learning more about dōTERRA and their CPTG® (certified pure, therapeutic grade) certification. I learned about what made these oils different, and I felt comfortable experimenting with internal usage with so many more oils than I had when using oils from other sources. My entire world of alchemy through mixology opened up, and I began to get really creative. I also opted to continue my education and became a certified health coach through the Institute for Integrative Nutrition.

I began integrating my love for healthy cooking with essential oils, and our kitchen became an overnight explosion of aromatic possibilities and flavor. I was churning out recipes infused with these amazing oils and creating food that not only had a beautiful flavor and aromatic quality but was also medicinally elevated. Salad dressings were becoming health tonics, dips and spreads were becoming immune boosters—I was really onto something here.

In time, my wife, Meredith, and I chose dōTERRA as our next venture and began building our own business. Our choice has proven to be extremely successful. In 2018, I was able to put my creativity to the page and published my first book, *The Essential Mixologist*, where I teach people how to infuse essential oils into cocktails, mocktails, and elixirs.

I am blessed to find true freedom as an alchemist, mixologist, and hobby chef. I believe that plants are here for many reasons and that they also want to come out and play with us in the world. They want to be a part of the conversation, on the dance floor, and at the dinner party. Incorporating essential oils into your kitchen (using only dōTERRA CPTG essential oils—because we know they are the best) is not only fun but is also actually good for you and good for your soul.

I am so excited to introduce you to these recipes. They are easy to make, fun to share, and delicious to eat. *The Essential Foodie* gives those of us who share essential oils already a wonderful roadmap to introduce them to new people, and it gives those of us who are always looking for ways to level up our kitchen creations an infusion of flavor you won't find elsewhere. And, of course, it give us ways to contribute to our overall health and wellness.

May the pages of this book open up your heart to the magic of the aromatic plant kingdom and the gift of essential oils. May you find their laughter in the wind, and may it invite your own laughter to play, dance, and feast with them in the most delicious ways!

FOOD IS *a Connective Tissue*

People simply don't connect in the same ways anymore. We bury our heads in our phones and surf around social media sites, trying to fill that innate human need—connection. I believe there is no replacement for the real thing, and I believe food—the act of cooking and eating together—can serve as a lifeline for us to connect to one another.

We gather in the kitchen. We cook, we eat, we talk, we laugh, and we share, all in the name of a meal. Food opens doors to cultures, ethnicities, and traditions. It provides the foundation for us to be with one another, belly to belly.

Several years ago, my mom and I prepared to celebrate Passover, the first major holiday since my dad had passed. Barely two months had gone by since we lost him, and things were still very tender.

We decided we would break from the tradition of cooking Ashkenazi cuisine, which comes from an eastern European influence, and instead cook Sephardic cuisine, connecting us to an entirely different lineage of our Jewish roots. Sephardic cuisine has a very Mediterranean influence; it emphasizes a lot of fresh salads and meats, incorporating dried fruits and other unique flavors. My dad didn't really care for this type of food. It's not that we didn't want to remember him—rather, the grief was still so raw for us that we wanted to bring in a new tradition that would allow us some space from how much we missed him.

Diving into these ingredients and new recipes helped my mom and me connect to something beyond our grief. While we were eating, we spoke about my dad and how we wished he were with us. We also laughed about how much he would have disliked the meal. It was truly a memorable meal that we shared together, and it turned out wonderfully.

I believe food is a connective tissue for humanity, a lifeline to one another and even to our country of origin. In a world weighed down by technology, food inspires conversation with each other and gives us an opportunity to create meaningful experiences together. It touches all of our senses and allows us to share something real with another human being.

In fact, as I add the finishing touches to this book, we are in the midst of a global pandemic, and these words ring true now more than ever. One of the many beautiful things I am witnessing at this time is a return to the kitchen, even if only by necessity. I see people gathering with one another to make their daily meals. Families are sitting down at the kitchen table together once again and sharing three meals a day—all made from scratch, the way a meal should be made.

Two of my greatest joys are essential oils and cooking. When we combine these things, the possibilities are endless. And when we add the people we love the most to this combination, the joy we experience is unlimited. The aromatic integration of essential oils into any recipe brings people together in ways I have never experienced before.

I invite you to use this book as a means of connecting more with people. Take the opportunity to cook together, eat together, and simply just be together. It's what the world needs right now.

A COLLISION *of Flavor and Wellness*

Essential oils are the most extraordinary ingredients I have ever worked with in my kitchen. For those unfamiliar with this ingredient, I'll give a brief overview. Essential oils are chemical compounds that are extracted from parts of plants and trees. They are the "essence" of the bark, flower, fruit, seed, or leaf that they are extracted from, and they are highly concentrated, potent, and aromatic. They add layers of flavor and a unique array of aromatics to any dish. If that isn't enough to entice you, they also offer a plethora of support to our physical, emotional, and spiritual well-being—an extra boost of wellness.

The concept of cooking with essential oils is fairly new to the culinary world, but the concept of using food to enhance wellness isn't. Hippocrates, considered to be the father of medicine, said, "Let food be thy medicine and medicine be thy food."

There are countless culinary enthusiasts, renowned chefs, and home chefs alike who practice this truth in their daily life. They cook with superfoods like spinach for its excellent source of vitamins and minerals. They use cacao, high in theobromine, to support cardiovascular health. They forage for mushrooms, which are high in an antioxidant called selenium and help to naturally boost the immune system, among other things. They use avocados, an extremely healthy fat that helps our body in myriad ways, including cancer prevention.

It's pretty simple. Food can be medicinal—when it's real food. Food can also be poison—when it's not real food. A saying to live by: "Eat plants, not things made in plants."

If we know that food can be medicinal, it's a true gift to have dozens of essential oils at your fingertips to use in your culinary creations. Let us be reminded of the role plants (spices) play in cooking. Essential oils are alive and carry the vibration of a particular plant. When essential oils are added to any recipe, the food comes alive with energy and story. It's not only a shortcut to the most pronounced flavor you will ever experience, but also a way to enhance your own health and well-being with every drop you infuse into your culinary creations.

THE dōTERRA *Difference*

You are going to learn a lot of fun recipes from this book, and you will get excited about the creative flavors and their medicinal properties. Chances are you will be so excited that you will want to get some essential oils and begin playing immediately. Before we begin this journey, it's critical that I am clear about this very important truth: Not all essential oils are created equal. If you take away anything from this book, this would be the best thing I could offer you.

When choosing essential oils, you want to make sure they have been created in ideal conditions to maximize their efficacy. Each essential oil has a unique chemical composition that should be preserved during the production process. If your essential oils are created in a way that compromises that chemical composition, they won't give you the expected benefit.

When you choose dōTERRA, you are choosing essential oils that are gently and carefully distilled from plants that have been patiently harvested for ideal extract composition and efficacy. dōTERRA essential oils are:

- Sourced ethically and sustainably, using growers and harvesters who grow plants specifically for the essential oil industry.

- Created using the best seeds, soils, and growing environment, so plants are grown and harvested in ideal conditions.

- Thoroughly tested to ensure that they aren't tainted or compromised during any part of production—from harvesting to transportation to extraction.

Now, let's talk about testing. Each dōTERRA essential oil is carefully and thoroughly tested using dōTERRA's strict Certified Pure Therapeutic Grade (CPTG) quality protocol. This protocol includes three rounds of testing to ensure that there are no impurities from production, there are no added ingredients that are harmful, and there is consistent purity for each batch of essential oils. When you choose dōTERRA, you know that you are getting the correct chemical composition for each essential oil and therefore the most effective and beneficial essential oil—every time.

THE dōTERRA DIFFERENCE

This may have been slightly more information than you require about essential oils, but my appreciation for the perfection dōTERRA supplies us with is something I felt could not be left out. There's a reason why, after using essential oils for over 20 years, I only use dōTERRA. Experienced essential oil users will immediately recognize the superior quality standard for naturally safe, purely effective, therapeutic-grade dōTERRA essential oils.

This wouldn't be complete without sharing how and why dōTERRA is truly the most unique essential oil company in the world: it's called Cō-Impact Sourcing®. Not only is Co-Impact Sourcing my favorite thing about dōTERRA, but it's also what makes this company an indisputable force of good on the planet.

Most large essential oil companies buy up land to mass-produce oils in environments where plants don't thrive. However, dōTERRA places enormous value on the expertise of farmers at the local level in places where plants thrive best.

Through the implementation of Co-Impact Sourcing, dōTERRA creates exclusive and responsible partnerships with these master artisans, providing opportunities for them to be sovereign, independent business owners with dōTERRA as a sourcing partner. When dōTERRA looks for sourcing partners, they deliberately choose places where individual, social, economic, and environmental well-being can be directly improved. The bonus here is that many of the plants used for essential oils grow in developing countries, and through this model, dōTERRA gets to have a massive impact.

The result is complete transparency in the supply chain and a far more superior product than the world has ever seen. From the seed to the bottle, everyone gets what they need and deserve, the earth included. It's a win, win, win, win, and the beat goes on.

Lemongrass farmers and harvesters in India

INGREDIENTS *Matter*

Using quality ingredients is the foundation for creating a dish worthy of putting into our body temples.

Throughout this book, I won't always specify to use the highest quality ingredients, since for me it is a given—I use only the best. Some people have told me that when they follow my recipes, the end result tastes different than what they have experienced when I make it. I always ask them: What brand of olive oil did you use? Did you choose free-range eggs, grass-fed meats, and organic vegetables? They all respond the same: They used mass-produced ingredients and did not choose fresh, quality ingredients.

There is an ongoing argument that eating organic costs more money. While this may be true, the question we need to be asking ourselves is whether we want to spend the money on the front end or the back end. If we continue polluting our bodies with toxic food, it will ultimately affect our health, and the cost of poor health far surpasses paying a little more for quality. Think of it as adding to your health insurance plan.

Joan Borysenko writes in her book *The Plant Plus Diet Solution* that the average family of four, eating an average Standard American Diet (SAD), loses a whopping $2,275 a year to food waste—food that simply doesn't get eaten. Her suggestion—and I concur—is to take that extra money and put it toward quality organic food.

Mitigate the loss by coming up with a better system so that no food goes to waste. Spend the money that would otherwise be thrown into the garbage on your own health. You are worth it.

I highly recommend and invite you to begin choosing organic, non-GMO, free-range, grass-fed, and all of the other "buzz" words that really aren't buzz words—they just represent real food. Please don't negate the importance of this; it will make all the difference in the end product, and it will make all the difference in your overall health.

THINK LIKE *a Purist*

When I think of the word pure, it conjures the notion of something that's unadulterated, free of contaminants, wholesome, and untainted. When I apply that to cooking, it becomes something made with these things in mind, with the idea of getting to the heart of the ingredient.

I feel blessed these principles were taught to me at a very young age. My mom loves to cook, and when I was growing up she was always trying to make our food as healthy as she knew how to at the time. I was one of those kids who had an "untradable" lunch. While the other kids got Wonder bread with peanut butter and fluff, Doritos, and Hostess CupCakes, I was stuck with last night's leftover chicken breast on whole-wheat bread with lettuce (always romaine I might add) and tomato, a granola bar, and an apple. Nobody ever wanted to trade anything from their junk-food lunch for what I had in my healthy lunch—it just wasn't going to happen.

At the time, this was upsetting to a young kid. But over time, I became grateful my mother cared about me enough to not feed me fake food. When we see one another, we not only cook, but we go to farmers markets and shop for the best ingredients—both our standards are pretty high these days.

Thinking like a purist means you are committed to using ingredients that are real and in their purest form: free from chemicals, pesticides, hormones, and anything artificial. If this doesn't come natural to you, it's never too late to learn something new. Here are some helpful tips to get you on the road to thinking like a purist.

- Choose free-range chicken, grass-fed meats, and fish that isn't mass-produced in fish farms.

- Choose eggs from free-range chickens.

- Choose dairy from cows that have not been given any growth hormones, especially RBST (an artificial growth hormone used in cows to increase milk production).

- Choose organic, non-GMO, first-cold-pressed cooking oils.

- Choose organic fruits and vegetables. Get to know lists like "The Dirty Dozen" and "The Clean Fifteen." Check them from time to time, since they can change.

- Stay away from mass-produced ingredients from the larger companies, unless they are organic. Whenever possible, always choose organic and non-GMO for any ingredient.

- Be aware of ingredients, such as high-fructose corn syrup; MSG; natural flavors (nothing natural about them); vegetable oils like cottonseed, palm, canola, and safflower; added sugar; added sodium; corn; and soy—to name a few.

- Stay away from traditional table salt. Get to know the healthier salts: Himalayan salt, Fleur de Sel, Celtic Sea Salt, Maldon salt, etc.

- Only use dōTERRA CPTG essential oils.

- Read labels. You would be surprised at what they call food.

A GUIDED *Invitation*

I wrote this book for you. It's not the bible of cooking with essential oils, and it's not a dogmatic recipe book either. It's really more of a guided invitation.

I'm an activator. I love to inspire people, ignite them with ideas, and provide a template for action. I have created these recipes because I feel they showcase the ingredients I have chosen in the best way possible for my palate. We are all created bio-individually, and what I think tastes good may not taste good to another. Where I like fish, someone else might prefer chicken or no meat at all. Where I have said to use wild orange essential oil, someone else may prefer lime essential oil or grapefruit essential oil. If you need to follow a recipe, these won't let you down. However, I give you permission to modify, and I ask you to give yourself permission to modify as well. Most importantly, have fun with the process.

Once you understand the basics of how to use essential oils to cook, you will have your own inspiration on how to incorporate them into your own unique recipes. Don't ever take my word for it—allow your creativity, needs, and flavor desires to win every time.

CREATE *for* YOUR AUDIENCE

These recipes can be made to share with family, with friends, at a party, or even when teaching an essential oils class. I have used essential oil-infused food to introduce many people to these gifts of the earth, and I have even attracted business partners from sharing in this way. It's fun to have a small group of people over who are interested in learning about the essential oils lifestyle or the business and provide them with a unique experience.

When hosting a curated experience for potential business partners, I usually start with an essential oil–infused beverage, served with one or two dishes from the "Tapas-Style Dips, Spreads, and Dollops" section of this book. I then serve several more tapas, one at a time, allowing my guests to have a curated tasting experience. While they feast in culinary delight, I educate them about the essential oils used in each dish and how they can also be applied to their daily health and wellness routine.

I also like doing team training gatherings, where a small group will come to our home and I will cook something for them to eat while we train and help them grow their business. The team always ends up being inspired with new ways they can share essential oil experiences with others, and most importantly, we all have a great time.

Remember, tapas don't need a rhyme or reason to be part of a tasting menu. The idea is you are taking a trip around the world with the intention of experiencing as many flavors as possible. However, there are ways to choreograph certain flavor profiles if you feel the need for continuity. That's why I have created some menu suggestions based on audience and intention.

AUTHOR'S WARNING TO READER

Infusing essential oils into your food will produce the most flavorful and aromatic dishes you have ever experienced. Side effects may include feelings of happiness and an overall sense of well-being.

Please note: Essential oils are potent. A little goes a very long way. When I suggest a drop, I mean a drop. Remember, you can't take away, but you can always add more later. You will be amazed by how much flavor is contained within each drop. Please start slowly and allow the plants to reveal themselves to you and your senses.

GET INSPIRED BY THE MENU IDEAS FOR DIFFERENT AUDIENCES ON THE FOLLOWING PAGES.

MENU IDEAS *for* DIFFERENT AUDIENCES

ESSENTIAL OILS CLASS

When I teach an essential oils class, I love to give people the experience of ingesting the oils. I keep the menu simple, easy, and cost-effective so that it's easy for my team to recreate. One food recipe item and one drink recipe are enough.

Superfood Spinach Pesto (page 69)
  or **Essential Hummus** (page 75)

Cucumber Cooler (page 157)

MENU IDEAS *for* DIFFERENT AUDIENCES

CURATED EXPERIENCE FOR A POTENTIAL BUSINESS PARTNER

I love showcasing the oils by curating a tasting experience for a potential business partner. It gives us space to connect and share an experience together. I usually plan to spend a couple of hours with my guests and take my time serving each taste. While they sip and snack, I educate them about the oils in each dish and talk about business opportunities.

WELCOME DRINK
Gin-less Juniper Spritz (page 161)

APPETIZER BOARD
Superfood Spinach Pesto (page 69)
Elevated Mango Salsa (page 79)
Aged cheddar topped with rosemary-infused blackberry jelly (page 64)

TAPAS (SERVED ONE AT A TIME)
Carrot, Apple, and Beet Salad with Turmeric Dressing (page 89)
Southeast Asian–Inspired Happy Soup (page 116)
Essential Orange Beef (page 108)

DESSERT
Tummy Tamer (page 155)
Bar of dark chocolate finished with lavender-infused Fleur de Sel (page 139)

MENU IDEAS *for* DIFFERENT AUDIENCES

TEAM MEETING

When I can gather my team in person, it's always fun to have them over for a training and incorporate an essential oil eating experience. It gives them ideas on how they can use and share the oils and also spoils them a little. A big pot of soup always hits the spot on these occasions.

WELCOME DRINK

Wake-Up Call Immune Booster (page 151)

APPETIZER BOARD

Roasted Baba Ganoush with Lemon and Coriander (page 72)
Essential Olive Tapenade (page 77)
Chill Dill-icious Dressing (page 47) with crudités

SOUP

Essential Roasted Garlic and Butternut Squash Soup (page 120)

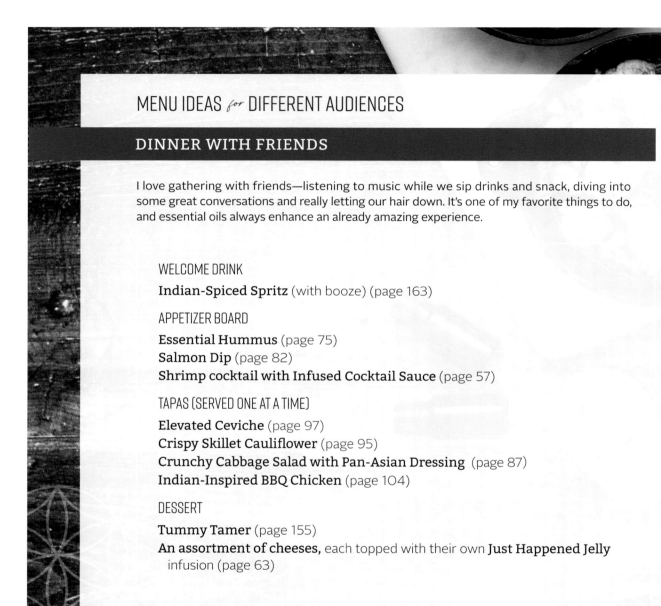

MENU IDEAS *for* DIFFERENT AUDIENCES

DINNER WITH FRIENDS

I love gathering with friends—listening to music while we sip drinks and snack, diving into some great conversations and really letting our hair down. It's one of my favorite things to do, and essential oils always enhance an already amazing experience.

WELCOME DRINK
Indian-Spiced Spritz (with booze) (page 163)

APPETIZER BOARD
Essential Hummus (page 75)
Salmon Dip (page 82)
Shrimp cocktail with Infused Cocktail Sauce (page 57)

TAPAS (SERVED ONE AT A TIME)
Elevated Ceviche (page 97)
Crispy Skillet Cauliflower (page 95)
Crunchy Cabbage Salad with Pan-Asian Dressing (page 87)
Indian-Inspired BBQ Chicken (page 104)

DESSERT
Tummy Tamer (page 155)
An assortment of cheeses, each topped with their own **Just Happened Jelly** infusion (page 63)

MENU IDEAS *for* DIFFERENT AUDIENCES

MEDITERRANEAN THEMED MENU

If you'd rather have a themed meal for continuity in taste, here is a suggested menu. You can easily choose different recipes to create other themed experiences as well.

APPETIZER BOARD

Roasted Baba Ganoush with Lemon and Coriander (page 72)
Superfood Spinach Pesto (page 69)
Essential Hummus (page 75)

TAPAS (SERVED ONE AT A TIME)

I Wish I Was Tuscan Bean Soup (page 127)
Crispy Skillet Smashed Potatoes (page 93)
Rustic Chicken and Wilted Spinach (page 106)
I'm 10% Greek Lamb Meatballs (page 112)
 with **Zesty Tzatziki with Spearmint** (page 71)

DRESSINGS, MARINADES, *and* CONDIMENTS

Most store-bought salad dressings, marinades, and condiments have way too many ingredients, many of which we can't even pronounce.

Preparing a homemade salad dressing is one of the easiest things to make happen in the kitchen and can also double as a marinade for any type of meat or vegetable. Infusing essential oils into your dressings is a great way to support overall wellness with very little effort. Not only will the flavor get kicked up about a hundred notches, but the aromatic integration will also be a totally unique and wonderful experience for the senses.

The same can be said about condiments. There are some good organic options on the market in a pinch, but when we want to control the amount of sugar and preservatives in our food supply, scratch-made is always a better choice.

I am a Mason jar girl. I make a lot of stuff in them and store a lot of food-stuff in them. I recommend making your dressing right in the jar and also using it to store in the fridge. If you find yourself making a few recipes at a time, create a label with the date so you know when it was made. Chances are you will rip through your supplies pretty quickly, but the good news is these can keep for at least a few weeks. Remember, essential oils act as a natural preservative and are used in many foods we buy from the grocery store for just that purpose.

Have fun and shake it up!

Photo courtesy of Julez Weinberg

FENNEL *and* WILD ORANGE DIGESTIVO DRESSING

MAKES 8 SERVINGS

What if your salad appetizer could lift your mood and set up your body's digestion for the rest of your meal? Not only is this salad dressing an aromatic flavor journey of the senses, but it also provides your body with major support for several key systems.

This dressing doubles especially well as a marinade for any type of fish or chicken.

INGREDIENTS

1 cup cold-pressed extra virgin olive oil
½ cup apple cider vinegar
2 tablespoons lemon juice
2 tablespoons Dijon mustard
1 tablespoon honey
salt & pepper to taste
2 drops dōTERRA fennel essential oil
4 drops dōTERRA wild orange essential oil

 Combine all ingredients together in a Mason jar, cover tightly, shake, and serve.

THE "DROP" DOWN

Fennel essential oil has a sweet, herbaceous aroma with a taste similar to licorice. It's a wonderful digestion aid and can be found in the foods of many cultures that use it for that purpose.

Wild orange essential oil has a bright, citrusy aroma and is very emotionally uplifting as well as energizing to the body and mind. When used internally, it's a wonderful support to both the immune system and digestive system and acts as an overall cleansing tonic. It's actually one of my favorite essential oils!

LEMONGRASS *and* GINGER PAN-ASIAN DRESSING

MAKES 8 SERVINGS

I'm an Asian fusion fanatic. I think the array of spices used in this part of the world are some of the most interesting to the palate. Remember, when we choose to use the essential oil instead of the dried botanical, it's a shortcut to gastronomy town with a boatload of health benefits.

This dressing doubles especially well as a marinade for any type of fish or meat, as well as a yummy sauce to use over veggies and rice bowls.

INGREDIENTS

1 cup cold-pressed sesame oil
½ cup rice wine vinegar
2 tablespoons tamari
   (can also use coconut aminos if soy-free)
2 tablespoons lime juice
1 tablespoon garlic sauce
   (cut in half to make it less spicy)
½ teaspoon fish sauce
   (omit to make it vegetarian/vegan)
1 tablespoon coconut sugar
2 drops dōTERRA ginger essential oil
2 drops dōTERRA lemongrass essential oil

THE "DROP" DOWN

Ginger essential oil has a spicy, earthy aroma that can be emotionally empowering to individuals feeling stuck. When ingested, it's the perfect digestion aid and can assist with various types of digestive discomfort, including sensitivity to motion while traveling.

Lemongrass essential oil has a herbaceous, citrus aroma that can be emotionally uplifting while also inspiring a positive outlook on life. When ingested, it promotes healthy digestion and acts as an overall tonic to the entire body.

 Combine all ingredients together in a Mason jar, cover tightly, shake, and serve.

ROSEMARY *and* LEMON DETOX DRESSING

MAKES 8 SERVINGS

We are bombarded by toxins on a daily basis: environmental toxins as well as toxins in our food, our water supply, and even in many of the products we use to take care of ourselves. Bottom line—we could all use a little support in this area. This simple, aromatic, and tasty salad dressing is the perfect addition to a weekly menu, and your body will thank you.

This dressing doubles especially well as a marinade for any type of fish, chicken, or pork.

INGREDIENTS

1 cup cold-pressed extra virgin olive oil
½ cup balsamic vinegar
1 tablespoon real maple syrup
1 teaspoon garlic powder
  (can also use 1 garlic clove, minced)
salt & pepper to taste
2 drops dōTERRA rosemary essential oil
4 drops dōTERRA lemon essential oil

 Combine all ingredients together in a Mason jar, cover tightly, shake, and serve.

THE "DROP" DOWN

Rosemary essential oil has a herbaceous and energizing aroma that assists with mental clarity. When used internally, it can assist the body's natural detoxification process, calm the nervous system, and aid digestion.

Lemon essential oil has a bright and citrusy aroma that's very energizing and has the ability to elevate one's mood. When taken internally, it aids with cleansing and detoxification and can also support healthy respiratory function.

CHILL *Dill-icious* DRESSING

MAKES 8-10 SERVINGS

I had been making this dressing for years before I decided to add a drop of lavender to it, and it changed everything! Among many things, lavender is very calming—hence the "chill" reference.

This dressing doubles especially well as a marinade for any type of fish or chicken. Here's a little tip: if you add ¼ cup of plain Greek yogurt, or any unsweetened plant-based yogurt, it makes an excellent dip for crudités.

INGREDIENTS

1 cup cold-pressed extra virgin olive oil
¼ cup apple cider vinegar
2 tablespoons honey
¼ cup dill, finely chopped
1 teaspoon garlic powder
salt & pepper to taste
1 drop dōTERRA lavender essential oil
4 drops dōTERRA lemon essential oil

 Combine all ingredients together in a Mason jar, cover tightly, shake, and serve.

THE "DROP" DOWN

Lavender essential oil has a light and floral aroma that's very calming to the nervous system. It can be used both aromatically and topically, but when used internally, it can reduce anxious feelings and ease feelings of tension. It can also promote a peaceful night's sleep.

Lemon essential oil has a bright and citrusy aroma that's very energizing and has the ability to elevate one's mood. When taken internally, it aids with cleansing and detoxification and can also support healthy respiratory function.

SKINNY *Girl* DRESSING

MAKES 8 SERVINGS

For those who are truly counting calories, watching sugar intake, and looking for a little metabolic support, this dressing will rock your world. It's bright, delicious, and a summer salad favorite. If you are an afternoon exerciser, try this on a salad for lunch, followed by a lot of water, and watch the pounds fall off.

INGREDIENTS

1 cup cold-pressed extra virgin olive oil
½ cup apple cider vinegar
1 tablespoon lemon juice
1 teaspoon liquid stevia
1 teaspoon garlic powder
  (can also use 1 garlic clove, minced)
½ teaspoon cayenne powder
½ cup parsley, finely chopped
salt & pepper to taste
10 drops dōTERRA grapefruit essential oil

THE "DROP" DOWN

Grapefruit essential oil has a bright and energizing aroma. It can be very uplifting and help increase motivation. When taken internally, it supports a healthy metabolism and helps the body release cellulite in stubborn areas.

Combine all ingredients together in a Mason jar, cover tightly, shake, and serve.

CREAMY *Turmeric* DRESSING

MAKES 8-10 SERVINGS

With all the wonderful research available on turmeric these days, healthy-minded peeps are trying to work it into all kinds of recipes. Turmeric can lower inflammation in the body, making it well worth the extra effort to add it to your daily diet. I think you will be surprised by how creamy and delicious this dressing is. It doubles especially well as a spread and makes an excellent dip for crudités.

INGREDIENTS

1 ripe avocado
½ cup cold-pressed extra virgin olive oil
¼ cup apple cider vinegar
1 garlic clove, minced
1 lemon, squeezed for juice
2 tablespoons raw honey
salt & pepper to taste
1-2 drops dŌTERRA turmeric essential oil

 Combine all ingredients in a Vitamix, blender, or food processor, then transfer to a Mason jar.

THE "DROP" DOWN

Turmeric essential oil has a spicy and earthy aroma. It has been a key botanical in Ayurveda, India's primary health philosophy. The aroma is very grounding and provides a sense of support to individuals when there is a lot of change or uncertainty. Turmeric essential oil has a myriad of benefits, from providing antioxidant and immune support to supporting healthy glucose and lipid metabolism. It's one of the many essential oils that provides endless benefits to our overall health and wellness when incorporated into a daily routine.

Essential KETCHUP

MAKES A SMALL MASON JAR

I have always been a condiment girl. I love to spread it on, adding a dollop here and a dollop there. Ketchup is one of those things we *think* we have to buy in a store. Truth be told, it's super easy to make, tastes a whole lot better when it's from your own kitchen, and packs some extra support when we add the essential oils. Know that restaurant ketchup will never stand up to what's in your fridge. Once you start making your own, you will never look back.

INGREDIENTS

1 can (6 oz) tomato paste
¼ cup water
¼ cup honey
¼ cup apple cider vinegar
¼ teaspoon garlic powder
¼ teaspoon onion powder
½ teaspoon salt
1 drop dōTERRA clove essential oil
1 drops dōTERRA black pepper essential oil

DIRECTIONS

Combine tomato paste, water, vinegar, garlic powder, onion powder, and salt in a saucepan. Whisk the mixture as you bring it to a boil.

Turn the heat to low, add honey, and whisk it into the mixture.

Turn the heat off and whisk in clove and black pepper essential oils.

 Transfer to a Mason jar and store in the refrigerator.

THE "DROP" DOWN

Clove essential oil has a very soothing, warm, and spicy aroma. It has very high antioxidant properties and can be a great support to the cardiovascular system as well as enhance immunity.

Black pepper essential oil has a very soothing aroma. It's very high in the chemistry that allows a high level of antioxidant support to the body. It also aids in digestion and supports healthy circulation. Due to its unique spectrum of aromatics, it acts as a wonderful enhancement to many dishes.

SCRATCH-MADE *Infused* AIOLI

MAKES A SMALL MASON JAR

Aioli is really just an elevated mayonnaise—a decadent spread or dipping sauce most of us think we can only have in a restaurant. I'm here to dispel that untruth and encourage you to step up to the plate. It's super easy to make at home from scratch, I promise! You can cheat and use store-bought mayonnaise, but the problem there is all of those not-so-good-for- you ingredients you will find, like; soy oil, canola oil, or one of the many less superior oils.

This recipe has a handful of ingredients and is made in a blender. The best part about it is you can choose one of many essential oils to infuse into your aioli depending on what kind of flavor palate you are creating. The possibilities are endless, and with each choice, you unlock new flavors and support for your body temple. Let's play!

INGREDIENTS

2 free-range egg yolks (room temperature)
½ cup cold-pressed extra virgin olive oil
1 tablespoon lemon juice
1 garlic cloved, minced
½ teaspoon Dijon mustard
salt & pepper to taste
1-2 drops dōTERRA essential oil of choice

Suggestions FROM JULEZ

Here are some essential oils I think work well: basil, black pepper, cilantro, coriander, lavender, lemon, oregano, pink pepper, rosemary, or thyme.

If using cilantro or oregano, only use 1 drop.

Lemon combines well with all of these oils, so feel free to combine a drop of lemon with your essential oil of choice.

DIRECTIONS

In a blender, gently whirl egg yolks, lemon juice, garlic, and mustard until combined.

On low speed, drizzle the oil in slowly, allowing it to fold itself into the mixture before adding more. As you add more oil, you can go a little more quickly, working up to a slow and steady stream.

As you add the oil, the mixture will thicken, changing from liquid into a creamy-looking spread. At this point, add your essential oil of choice and season to taste with salt and pepper.

If the final product is too thick, thin it out with a couple drops of lemon juice. Make sure you don't use additional olive oil, because oil makes the aioli thicker.

 Serve right away, or cover and refrigerate. Will keep for up to two days.

Infused COCKTAIL SAUCE

MAKES A SMALL MASON JAR

I will say the same about the cocktail sauce as I said about the ketchup: another super easy thing to whip up on your own that tastes so much better than anything you would buy in a store, minus all those ingredients you can't pronounce.

INGREDIENTS

1 cup Essential Ketchup
   (can use regular organic ketchup)
1 tablespoon horseradish
1 tablespoon hot sauce of choice
4 drops dōTERRA lemon essential oil
2 drops dōTERRA black pepper essential oil

 Combine all ingredients together in a Mason jar, cover tightly, shake, and serve.

THE "DROP" DOWN

Lemon essential oil has a bright and citrusy aroma that's very energizing and has the ability to elevate one's mood. When taken internally, it aids with cleansing and detoxification and can also support healthy respiratory function.

Black pepper essential oil has a very soothing aroma. It's very high in the chemistry that allows a high level of antioxidant support to the body. It also aids in digestion and supports healthy circulation. Due to its unique spectrum of aromatics, it acts as a wonderful enhancement to many dishes.

Essential MAPLE-BOURBON BBQ SAUCE

MAKES A SMALL MASON JAR

I love homemade BBQ sauce! Barbecue sauce out of a bottle is sacrilegious. I mean, it's just not right! Depending on where you are in the United States, the BBQ sauce changes quite a bit. You've got your mustard base, vinegary, sweet & tangy, and smokey & spicy—to name a few. I actually really like them all, but this one is a sure crowd-pleaser every time.

This sauce goes well on everything—pork, chicken, burgers, shrimp, tofu, tempeh—and even makes a great dipping sauce for sweet potato or regular fries.

INGREDIENTS

1 can (6 oz) tomato paste
¼ cup water
2 tablespoons Dijon mustard
¼ cup bourbon
¼ cup maple syrup
¼ cup molasses
¼ teaspoon garlic powder
¼ teaspoon onion powder
¼ teaspoon cumin
½ teaspoon salt
1 drop dōTERRA clove essential oil
2 drops dōTERRA black pepper essential oil

DIRECTIONS

Combine everything except the essential oils in a saucepan.

Whisk the mixture together as you bring it to a boil, then turn the heat to low and let simmer for 15-20 minutes, stirring occasionally while the bourbon burns off.

Turn the heat off, add clove and black pepper essential oils, and mix together.

 Whisk, transfer to a Mason jar, and store in the refrigerator.

THE "DROP" DOWN

Clove essential oil has a very soothing, warm, and spicy aroma. It has very high antioxidant properties and can be a great support to the cardiovascular system as well as enhance immunity.

Black pepper essential oil has a very soothing aroma. It's very high in the chemistry that allows a high level of antioxidant support to the body. It also aids in digestion and supports healthy circulation. Due to its unique spectrum of aromatics, it acts as a wonderful enhancement to many dishes.

Essential LEMON TAHINI SAUCE

MAKES A SMALL MASON JAR

One of the secrets to having great-tasting, healthy food available at all times is preparation. The right sauces already made and ready to use will make the difference between a delicious rice and veggie bowl, salad, or sandwich and a mediocre one every time. Everyone needs a jar of this in their refrigerator, ready to go. It's great on so many dishes, brightens up the palate, and even lifts your mood.

INGREDIENTS

¾ cup tahini paste
¼ cup water
2 garlic cloves, minced
¼ teaspoon salt
4 drops dōTERRA lemon essential oil

DIRECTIONS

Place all ingredients in a mixing bowl and gently whisk until blended. (Using a blender makes the paste too thick, and it can become like a nut butter instead of a sauce.)

 Transfer to a Mason jar and store in the refrigerator.

THE "DROP" DOWN

Lemon essential oil has a bright and citrusy aroma that's very energizing and has the ability to elevate one's mood. When taken internally, it aids with cleansing and detoxification and can also support healthy respiratory function.

JUST *Happened* JELLY

MAKES A SMALL MASON JAR

We were on the tail end of being in quarantine for several months when I asked Meredith what she wanted for lunch. She replied, "A good old-fashioned peanut butter and jelly sandwich." Happy to oblige, I made my way downstairs and quickly realized we didn't have any jelly. At the time, it wasn't that easy to just run to the store. So, I did what I always do in these situations. I got creative. I knew I had plenty of frozen berries in the freezer and a willingness to play in the kitchen. Ten minutes later, I had the most delicious wild orange–infused blueberry jelly I have ever tasted. I will never buy jelly in the store again.

Since then, I have experimented with so many flavors, and the results are delightful each time. Jelly is not only for peanut butter sandwiches and toast; it can also be drizzled on most cheeses, added to a grilled cheese sandwich, used as a spread on other sandwiches, and used to replace syrup on pancakes and French toast. I could go on and on about how to use homemade essential oil–infused jelly to elevate your culinary creations—maybe I'll write a follow-up book on it. Until then, here's the recipe and a few other fun infusion ideas.

INGREDIENTS

1 cup frozen blueberries (fresh if you have them)
1 tablespoon maple syrup
1 teaspoon arrowroot powder
2 drops dōTERRA wild orange essential oil

THE "DROP" DOWN

Wild orange essential oil has a bright, citrusy aroma and is very emotionally uplifting as well as energizing to the body and mind. When used internally, it's a wonderfulsupport to both the immune system and digestive system and acts as an overall cleansing tonic. It's actually one of my favorite essential oils!

DIRECTIONS

Place blueberries and maple syrup in a medium saucepan. Whisk over medium heat for about five minutes, until the blueberries break down.

Add arrowroot powder and continue whisking until the mix thickens into a jelly-like consistency.

Turn the heat off and whisk in wild orange essential oil. If the mixture becomes too thick, add a little water.

 Let it cool, transfer to a Mason jar, and store in the refrigerator.

Suggestions FROM JULEZ

Here are a few other ideas to get your creativity flowing. Use the same method as Just Happened Jelly each time and be inspired to make your own blend—I bet it will be amazing! Remember, the process will always be the same, so follow the previous recipe's instructions.

Strawberry Jelly with 1 drop dōTERRA black pepper essential oil

Delicious on a grilled cheese sandwich.

Blackberry Jelly with 1 drop dōTERRA rosemary essential oil

Delicious on top of Brie, aged cheddar, or goat cheese, served with crackers.

Blueberry Jelly with 1 drop dōTERRA lavender essential oil

Delicious on top of Brie, aged cheddar, or goat cheese, served with crackers.

Cranberry Jelly with 1 drop dōTERRA thyme essential oil

Delicious on a turkey sandwich.

Blueberry Jelly with 1 drop dōTERRA ginger essential oil

Delicious on pancakes or French toast.

TAPAS-STYLE DIPS, SPREADS, and DOLLOPS

My absolute favorite way to eat is when I can share my food with others. I love to pick, dip, and spread a dollop of this and a dollop of that on my plate.

If you were invited to my home for "happy hour," it's very likely that several of the recipes in this chapter would make an appearance. I'd use one of my oversized serving boards to present a variety of little white bowls for these tasty dips accompanied by a variety of accoutrements. Tiny spoons or small spreading knives would be tucked into each of the bowls for ease, and small plates would provide you with your very own little mixing station.

We would sit, sip, and snack together while we talked. If it's your first time, chances are you will keep asking, "Only one drop of (fill in the essential oil) is in here? Really? That's all?"

The food would be yummy, but the essential oils would be the star of the show. They always are.

Superfood SPINACH PESTO

MAKES 8-10 SERVINGS

This is one of my favorite culinary inventions! It's a staple in our kitchen. When one batch runs out, another is whipped up within a day or two. The best thing about this recipe is that it's spinach! Every time you dip, spread, or dollop, you are getting a wonderful serving of spinach. Popeye would be proud! It tastes so good, even the kiddos love it!

Using spinach instead of basil makes this an easy pesto to have around all year. It also elevates the nutrition factor and prolongs freshness (basil tends to brown very easily once cut). Oh, and feel free to change up the nuts. I use whatever I have around: walnuts, cashews, pecans, pumpkin seeds, sunflower seeds, almonds—they all work!

INGREDIENTS

4 cups spinach (baby spinach works best)
½ cup cold-pressed extra virgin olive oil
2 garlic cloves
1 cup raw walnuts (feel free to change up
   the nuts)
salt & pepper to taste
1 drop dōTERRA basil essential oil
3 drops dōTERRA lemon essential oil

 Serve in your favorite bowl. This makes a great spread for sandwiches and paninis and can be added to a homemade pizza and even tossed with pasta. Get creative!

DIRECTIONS

Combine spinach, olive oil, garlic, salt, pepper, and basil and lemon essential oils in a food processor or Vitamix. Blend until the mixture is course (pasty, not liquid).

Add the nuts last and pulse so they stay chunky and add texture.

THE "DROP" DOWN

Basil essential oil has a very herbaceous and refreshing aroma. It is a wonderful support to the body regarding inflammation and has an energizing and restorative quality.

Lemon essential oil has a bright and citrusy aroma that's very energizing and has the ability to elevate one's mood. When taken internally, it aids with cleansing and detoxification and can also support healthy respiratory function.

ZESTY TZATZIKI *with* SPEARMINT

MAKES 8-10 SERVINGS

Is it a dip, marinade, or condiment? In my experience, it's all three and more. Tzatziki is one of those things that seems too exotic to tackle in your own kitchen. In actuality, it couldn't be any easier. A fresh batch of this is a usual suspect in our fridge. It's the perfect dip for fresh veggies or warm pita. It's also very convenient to smother over chicken or spice up a homemade lamb burger. The kick of spearmint makes it extra special and gives the body some additional digestive support!

INGREDIENTS

2 cups Greek yogurt
1 cucumber, peeled, seeded, and chopped
½ cup cold-pressed extra virgin olive oil
2 tablespoons lemon juice
2 garlic cloves
½ cup dill, finely chopped
salt & pepper to taste
2 drops dōTERRA spearmint essential oil

DIRECTIONS

Combine Greek yogurt, cucumber, olive oil, lemon juice, and garlic in a food processor and pulse until the mixture is smooth but has enough small chunks of cucumber to provide texture (you can also set aside some of the cucumber and fold it in later for extra texture).

Transfer the mixture into a mixing bowl. Fold in dill, salt, pepper, and spearmint essential oil.

 Serve in your favorite bowl with a drizzle of olive oil on top. This makes a nice addition to lamb and chicken dishes.

THE "DROP" DOWN

Spearmint essential oil has a refreshing, sweet aroma that's very emotionally uplifting. When taken internally, it can aid in digestion and assist with an upset stomach.

ROASTED BABA GANOUSH
with CORIANDER *and* LEMON

MAKES 8 SERVINGS

A couple of years ago, Meredith bought me a DNA test as a gift. It was no surprise to find out I have Greek, Middle Eastern, and North African blood coursing through my veins. It explained my love for mezze, a spread of small dishes served as appetizers or tapas in these parts of the world. When I talk about food being a connective tissue, sharing tapas with people you love is a wonderful example. Baba ganoush is another perfect dippy-tapas-style recipe that's super easy to whip up and a definite crowd-pleaser.

INGREDIENTS

1 large eggplant
½ cup cold-pressed extra virgin olive oil
½ cup tahini
1 garlic clove
½ cup parsley, chopped
¼ teaspoon cumin
½ teaspoon smoked paprika
salt & pepper to taste
1 drop dōTERRA coriander essential oil
4 drops dōTERRA lemon essential oil
Pinch of smoked paprika

THE "DROP" DOWN

Coriander essential oil has a wonderful and unique aromatic that's very green and herbaceous with a touch of a floral note. Adding this into any dish helps the body's digestion.

Lemon essential oil has a bright and citrusy aroma that's very energizing and has the ability to elevate one's mood. When taken internally, it aids with cleansing and detoxification and can also support healthy respiratory function.

DIRECTIONS

Preheat the oven to 450° F.

Line a baking sheet with foil or parchment paper to prevent eggplant from sticking.

Cut the eggplant in half and brush with olive oil and salt. Place it skin-side down on the baking sheet and roast for 40-45 minutes, until the interior is tender and the skin looks loose. When finished, set aside to cool.

Scoop the eggplant from the skin and place in a bowl. Discard the skins.

Add olive oil, garlic, cumin, smoked paprika, salt, and pepper. Mix vigorously until eggplant breaks down. Fold in tahini, parsley, and coriander and lemon essential oils. Mix well.

 Serve in your favorite bowl with a drizzle of olive oil and a pinch of smoked paprika on top for color. This goes well with warm pita, crusty bread, gluten-free crackers, or sliced veggies.

Essential HUMMUS

MAKES 8-10 SERVINGS

Hummus is a staple to any mezze spread. Most of the store-bought options have way too many ingredients in them, including oils that shouldn't be in there, like canola or safflower oil. Making homemade hummus is easy, healthier, more cost-effective, and delicious. Feel free to use dry garbanzo beans that you soak overnight, but for the ease of this recipe you can also open a can of organic ones.

INGREDIENTS

1 can (15 oz) garbanzo beans
¼ cup cold-pressed extra virgin olive oil
¼ cup tahini
1 garlic clove
¼ teaspoon cumin
½ teaspoon salt
2 drops dōTERRA lemon essential oil
1 drop dōTERRA black pepper essential oil
1 drop dōTERRA coriander essential oil

DIRECTIONS

Drain the garbanzo beans and combine all ingredients in a Vitamix, food processor, or blender. Blend thoroughly until creamy.

THE "DROP" DOWN

Lemon essential oil has a bright and citrusy aroma that's very energizing and has the ability to elevate one's mood. When taken internally, it aids with cleansing and detoxification and can also support healthy respiratory function.

Black pepper essential oil has a very soothing aroma. It's very high in the chemistry that allows a high level of antioxidant support to the body. It also aids in digestion and supports healthy circulation. Due to its unique spectrum of aromatics, it acts as a wonderful enhancement to many dishes.

Coriander essential oil has a wonderful and unique aromatic that's very green and herbaceous with a touch of a floral note. Adding this into any dish helps the body's digestion.

 Serve in your favorite bowl with a drizzle of olive oil and cracked black pepper on top.

Essential OLIVE TAPENADE

MAKES 8 SERVINGS

Tapenade is usually a finely chopped or puréed spread made primarily of olives, capers, and anchovies. The word *tapenade* is actually derived from the Provence word for capers. My approach to food is always about simplicity, and while I love capers and anchovies, they aren't something that everyone always stocks in the pantry. I also think the combination can sometimes be a little on the salty side.

My version of tapenade leaves out the capers and anchovies, making it vegetarian friendly and lower in sodium. If you are a texture person and like the chunk factor, go with my suggestions to chop. If you prefer a more spreadable version, place the ingredients into a Vitamix, food processor, or blender. Either way, this stuff is divine and makes a great addition to any cheese plate, charcuterie plate, or veggie tapas plate.

INGREDIENTS

2 cups kalamata olives, finely chopped
¼ cup cold-pressed extra virgin olive oil
2 garlic cloves, minced
½ cup parsley, chopped
1 teaspoon black pepper
1-2 drops dōTERRA fennel essential oil
3 drops dōTERRA lemon essential oil

 Serve in your favorite bowl with crusty bread or gluten-free crackers.

DIRECTIONS

Combine all ingredients in a mixing bowl and stir thoroughly.

THE "DROP" DOWN

Fennel essential oil has a sweet, herbaceous aroma with a taste similar to licorice. It's a wonderful digestion aid and can be found in the foods of many cultures that use it for that purpose.

Lemon essential oil has a bright and citrusy aroma that's very energizing and has the ability to elevate one's mood. When taken internally, it aids with cleansing and detoxification and can also support healthy respiratory function.

Elevated MANGO SALSA

MAKES A LARGE MASON JAR

I'm a salsa junkie. I mean, I seriously love the stuff. Salsa has a certain life force; it's bright, fresh, colorful, and full of flavor. It's really hard for me to understand how or why anyone would ever consider opening a jar of salsa when it's so easy to make your own and the results are a billion times better than store-bought. We have traveled to Mexico many times, and one of my favorite things to taste there is all the unique salsas (well, that and the tequila and mezcal, haha).

Salsa is a saucy condiment made from fresh ingredients with an unlimited amount of ways to be expressed through our own creativity. My experience in Mexico and with friends indigenous to the culture has taught me that no two salsas are the same. Salsa is a personal thumbprint of flavor expression, and I hope you enjoy mine.

INGREDIENTS

1 can (28 oz) crushed tomatoes
1 small red onion, finely chopped
1 large mango, diced (can use 2 cups frozen
   if fresh isn't available)
1 jalapeño pepper, finely chopped
1 habanero pepper, finely chopped
1 lime, squeezed for juice
½ cup cilantro, chopped
¼ teaspoon cumin
½ teaspoon salt
1 drop dōTERRA cilantro essential oil
2 drops dōTERRA lime essential oil

 Transfer to a Mason jar and store in the refrigerator. The salsa keeps for 7-10 days.

DIRECTIONS

Combine all ingredients in a large mixing bowl. Allow the flavors to marinade with one another for at least a few hours.

Serve in your favorite bowl with high-quality tortilla chips.

THE "DROP" DOWN

Cilantro essential oil has a very fresh, bright, and herbal aromatic. When used internally, it promotes healthy digestion, supports a good immune system response, and nourishes the nervous system. Cilantro is also known for its ability to aid the body's detox response to heavy metals through chelation.

Lime essential oil has an uplifting and energizing aroma and adds a bright, citrusy flavor to food. Its purifying qualities make it a wonderful support to the body's internal cleansing process. When taken internally, it provides support to the immune system.

Gold MEDALIST GUACAMOLE

MAKES 6-8 SERVINGS

Every summer my cousins host an annual guac-off party at their home. It's a foodie bash with a built-in guacamole competition, legit judges, prizes, and prestige. Winning the gold medal at one of these parties gives a person authentic bragging rights. Several years ago, I won—and this is my recipe.

INGREDIENTS

4 perfectly ripe avocados
1 small red onion, finely chopped
¼ cup cilantro, chopped
1 regular-sized jalapeño pepper, finely chopped
1 garlic clove, minced
1 lime, squeezed for juice
¼ teaspoon cumin powder
½ teaspoon Himalayan salt
1 drop dōTERRA lime essential oil

DIRECTIONS

Add minced garlic to a large metal bowl. Mix it around the bowl so the oils from the garlic cover some of the inside. Once coated, discard the rest of the garlic, leaving only the oil residue behind.

Scoop three of the ripe avocados into the bowl and carefully smash them with a fork. The consistency should be chunky, not creamy.

Dice the fourth avocado into small cubes and set it aside.

Combine the rest of the ingredients and gently fold them into the mashed avocados—technique goes a long way in this step.

Gently fold the diced avocado into the mixture.

THE "DROP" DOWN

Lime essential oil has an uplifting and energizing aroma and adds a bright, citrusy flavor to food. Its purifying qualities make it a wonderful support to the body's internal cleansing process. When taken internally, it provides support to the immune system.

SALMON *Dip*

MAKES 8-10 SERVINGS

I have tasted so many store-bought salmon dips loaded with things that just don't need to be in there. On top of that, the quality of the salmon is always questionable and most likely farm-raised—another big no-no when we are coming from a purist perspective. Not to mention that the price per pound is usually absurd. Here we have a simple-to-make recipe, using fresh ingredients enhanced with beautiful essential oils. If you take the time to make this, I can almost promise that you will never buy it in a store again. It will become one of those snacks that finds a permanent spot in your rotation.

INGREDIENTS

1 pound fresh salmon
1 teaspoon smoked paprika
salt & pepper to taste
1 cup Greek yogurt
¼ cup dill, chopped
¼ cup scallions, chopped
1 tablespoon Dijon mustard
1 drop dōTERRA black pepper essential oil
1 drop dōTERRA pink pepper essential oil
2 drops dōTERRA lemon essential oil

THE "DROP" DOWN

Black pepper essential oil has a very soothing aroma. It's very high in the chemistry that allows a high level of antioxidant support to the body. It also aids in digestion and supports healthy circulation. Due to its unique spectrum of aromatics, it acts as a wonderful enhancement to many dishes.

Pink pepper essential oil has a slightly spicy and fruity aroma. Taking this oil internally supports the immune system and digestive system and helps the body maintain healthy cellular function.

Lemon essential oil has a bright and citrusy aroma that's very energizing and has the ability to elevate one's mood. When taken internally, it aids with cleansing and detoxification and can also support healthy respiratory function.

DIRECTIONS

Preheat the oven to 350° F.

Place the salmon in a cast-iron skillet, skin down. Season the top with smoked paprika, salt, and pepper.

Place the skillet in the oven and cook for 20 minutes. After 20 minutes, flip the salmon and place it back in the oven skin-side up for 10 more minutes.

Remove the salmon from the oven and pull the skin off the bottom. (You can eat the skin as a snack—salmon skin is delicious and very good for you.)

Set the salmon aside in a prep bowl and allow to cool for 20 minutes. While the salmon is cooling, place the rest of the ingredients in a large mixing bowl.

Once the salmon has cooled, take a fork and separate it in the same way you would a can of tuna fish.

Add the salmon to the rest of the ingredients. Mix thoroughly, but make sure the salmon is still chunky. Add more salt to taste.

 Serve in your favorite bowl with any type of cracker or toast points, or sliced cucumbers.

TAPAS-STYLE FLEXITARIAN, DISHES (VEGGIES, SEAFOOD, POULTRY, *and* MEAT)

Here we have a diverse series of recipes that allows for choices based on everyone's unique eating habits. The vision for me is always providing an experience where I am engaging with people when I eat. Therefore, tapas seem to be the best way to go.

I usually follow an 80/20 rule with my eating regimen. This means about eighty percent of my food is plant-based and the other twenty percent is sustainably-and ethically-sourced animal protein. A typical meal for me on the plate would consist of vegetables; fat from avocados, nuts, olive oil, etc.; and enough protein to fit into the palm of my hand. There are also days where one, two, or all of my meals are fully vegan. Or, when I eat pizza for lunch and a burger for dinner—it happens on occasion. It's really a personal choice based on what you feel your body needs. Some people require different foods with the changing seasons. It's important to honor your body and what you feel it needs to thrive.

A meal experience from this chapter might consist of three or four plates total, creating a tasting experience that people can slowly share with one another. You may find it fun to choose two or three veggie plates with one protein plate. Whatever you end up choosing, I'm sure you will find something here to delight your taste buds, senses, and, of course, provide that extra support to your overall well-being.

Crunchy CABBAGE SALAD *with* PAN-ASIAN DRESSING

MAKES 8-10 SERVINGS

Here's where things get fun. I'm all about creating ease in the kitchen and providing ways to use what you have. If by now you have fallen in love with creating your own salad dressings and you happen to have some of the Lemongrass and Ginger Pan-Asian Dressing sitting in the fridge, this will be super easy. If not, all you need to do is follow the recipe for that dressing and then add it to this one.

This is one of my favorite salads. It can be served as a stand-alone or used as a side dish. It seems the longer it sits in the refrigerator, the yummier it gets. So, feel free to double the recipe so you have extra.

INGREDIENTS

½ head savoy cabbage, thinly sliced
½ head red cabbage, thinly sliced
6 green scallions, thinly sliced
½ cup cilantro, chopped
½ cup sliced almonds
Lemongrass and Ginger Pan-Asian Dressing
  (page 43)
1 tablespoon Sriracha sauce (optional)

DIRECTIONS

Place all ingredients in a large mixing bowl.

Add an appropriate amount of Lemongrass and Ginger Pan-Asian Dressing (less if you like it dry, more if you like it wet).

THE "DROP" DOWN

Ginger essential oil has a spicy, earthy aroma that can be emotionally empowering to individuals feeling stuck. When ingested, it's the perfect digestion aid and can assist with various types of digestive discomfort, including sensitivity to motion while traveling.

Lemongrass essential oil has a herbaceous, citrus aroma that can be emotionally uplifting while also inspiring a positive outlook on life. When ingested, it promotes healthy digestion and acts as an overall tonic to the entire body.

 Toss thoroughly and serve. If you like things spicy, add 1 tablespoon Sriracha sauce when tossing.

CARROT, APPLE, *and* BEET SALAD *with* CREAMY TURMERIC DRESSING

MAKES 6-8 SERVINGS

Here's another recipe hack. I adore this salad. It's a dish that stands alone and can also be served as a side. If you have the Creamy Turmeric Dressing sitting in your fridge already, this will be a sinch. If not, follow the recipe for the dressing and then add to this salad.

INGREDIENTS

2 large beets, peeled and roughly chopped
2 large carrots, peeled and roughly chopped
2 Granny Smith apples, cored and
   roughly chopped
½ cup parsley, chopped
½ cup walnuts, chopped
Creamy Turmeric Dressing (page 51)

DIRECTIONS

Shred beets, carrots, and apples in a Vita mix or food processor.

Place the mixture in a large mixing bowl. Add parsley and walnuts.

THE "DROP" DOWN

Turmeric essential oil has a spicy and earthy aroma. It has been a key botanical in Ayurveda, India's primary health philosophy. The aroma is very grounding and provides a sense of support to individuals when there is a lot of change or uncertainty. Turmeric essential oil has a myriad of benefits, from providing antioxidant and immune support to supporting healthy glucose and lipid metabolism. It's one of the many essential oils that provides endless benefits to our overall health and wellness when incorporated into a daily routine.

 Cover with Creamy Turmeric Dressing and mix thoroughly.

Brown BUTTER SKILLET MUSHROOMS

MAKES 4-6 SERVINGS

Mushrooms are culinary creatures of the earth, powerful and mysterious. They have exquisite texture, flavor, and substance on the plate, and on the palate. Therefore, I believe they make the perfect "stand-alone" tapas dish to share with friends. There are many culinary marriages made in heaven, butter and mushrooms being one of them. Don't hold back on this ingredient—go all in and allow yourself to be delighted.

INGREDIENTS

1 pound cremini mushrooms, sliced ¼-inch thick
2 large shallots, halved and thinly sliced
3 tablespoons butter
½ teaspoon salt
¼ teaspoon ground black pepper
¼ cup parsley, finely chopped
1 drop dōTERRA clary sage essential oil

THE "DROP" DOWN

Clary sage essential oil has a woody, herbal aroma. When taken internally as well as used aromatically, it has a very calming effect on the psyche, promotes relaxation, and can contribute to a restful night's sleep.

DIRECTIONS

In a large cast-iron skillet over medium-high heat, melt butter and let it sizzle until it turns a light golden-brown.

Add mushrooms, shallots, salt, and pepper, stirring until completely coated with butter.

Sauté mushrooms and shallots for about 10-12 minutes, stirring often, until they are a deep-brown color. One key to mushrooms is to make sure they have enough space in the pan so they are not crowding one another.

Once the mushrooms are browned, add clary sage essential oil on the side of the skillet where the butter has puddled, then stir the contents thoroughly. Sauté for another 2-3 minutes.

Turn heat off and stir in parsley.

 Transfer to your favorite bowl and serve immediately, since they are best when still hot off the skillet.

CRISPY SKILLET *Smashed* POTATOES

MAKES 4-6 SERVINGS

I have to give my cousin Shelly credit for this idea. Over the years I have made it my own, but she was the initiator. The simplicity of the cooking method will have your guests thinking you are a kitchen magician. And the addition of the rosemary essential oil will have your guests thinking you are a culinary genius. Don't underestimate the power of the potato!

INGREDIENTS

10 small Yukon gold potatoes
½ cup cold-pressed extra virgin olive oil
½ cup scallions, thinly sliced
¼ teaspoon garlic powder
¼ teaspoon onion powder
salt & pepper to taste
1 drop dōTERRA rosemary essential oil

THE "DROP" DOWN

Rosemary essential oil has a herbaceous and energizing aroma that assists with mental clarity. When used internally, it can assist the body's natural detoxification process, calm the nervous system, and aid digestion.

DIRECTIONS

Preheat the oven to 425° F.

Parboil potatoes for approximately 10-12 minutes, until soft enough to stick a fork through but not fully cooked.

Coat cast-iron skillet with some of the olive oil.

Pour the rest of the olive oil in a separate bowl. Add rosemary essential oil to the bowl, mix thoroughly, and set aside for later.

When the potatoes are done, drain them and place them in the cast-iron skillet next to one another. Use a water glass or something flat and heavy to gently smash each potato into the skillet until they cover the surface area completely.

Drizzle almost all of the olive oil mixture (leave a little for later) over the potatoes, and sprinkle garlic power, onion powder, salt, and pepper evenly over them. Place the skillet in the oven for 30 minutes.

On the side, toss the scallions with the rest of the olive oil mixture. After 30 minutes, add the scallions on top of the potatoes and cook for another 10 minutes until everything is golden brown.

 Remove the skillet from the oven and serve hot. Potatoes will be extra crispy on the bottom, so use a flat-top spatula to serve.

Photo courtesy of Julez Weinberg

CRISPY *Skillet* CAULIFLOWER

MAKES 4-6 SERVINGS

I think cauliflower is one of the most delicious roasted vegetables. When done correctly, it tastes like savory candy. This dish has so much flavor, and with the cashews, so much texture. Using a cast- iron skillet with this recipe gives the cauliflower that beautiful and delicious sear we all love. If you really like cauliflower and don't have a cast-iron skillet, invest in one. They are not expensive and will make the results of this dish restaurant quality.

INGREDIENTS

1 large head of cauliflower, cut into bite-sized florets
½ cup cold-pressed extra virgin olive oil
½ teaspoon garlic powder
½ teaspoon cumin powder
½ teaspoon black pepper
½ teaspoon salt
½ cup raw cashews
1 drop dōTERRA pink pepper essential oil
1 drop dōTERRA turmeric essential oil
¼ cup parsley, chopped, for garnish

DIRECTIONS

Preheat the oven to 425° F.

Put olive oil in a large mixing bowl. Add pink pepper and turmeric essential oils. Blend thoroughly.

Toss cauliflower with the olive oil mixture. Add garlic powder, cumin powder, salt, and pepper. Make sure everything is coated evenly.

Place the mixture in a cast-iron skillet, making sure the cauliflower isn't too cramped. Place in the oven for 30 minutes or until golden brown.

THE "DROP" DOWN

Pink pepper essential oil has a slightly spicy and fruity aroma. Taking this oil internally supports the immune system and digestive system and helps the body maintain healthy cellular function.

Turmeric essential oil has a spicy and earthy aroma. It has been a key botanical in Ayurveda, India's primary health philosophy. The aroma is very grounding and provides a sense of support to individuals when there is a lot of change or uncertainty. Turmeric essential oil has a myriad of benefits, from providing antioxidant and immune support to supporting healthy glucose and lipid metabolism. It's one of the many essential oils that provides endless benefits to our overall health and wellness when incorporated into a daily routine.

 When finished, remove from the oven, place in your favorite bowl, garnish with parsley, drizzle a little olive oil on top, and serve.

MUSSELS *My Way*

MAKES 4 SERVINGS

My mom and I love eating mussels together, so when she visits, I always make them for us. Mussels are an interactive meal; opening up the shells, scooping up the juices, and finally slurping out the mussel is an eating sport. It's fun to watch the empty shells pile up in the discard bowl.

Mussels are indeed delicious, but they must be fresh—no exceptions. Make sure you buy them from a local fish store and only buy them if they are alive. When you get home, give them a good scrub and be sure to de-beard them (look for the little hairlike "beard" sticking out of the shell and pull it out). When you are done cooking the mussels, if one doesn't open, don't eat it. It usually means it wasn't alive to begin with. If you accidentally eat one like that, we have an essential oil that can help, so don't be intimidated—they are worth the extra effort.

INGREDIENTS

2 pounds mussels, cleaned and de-bearded
4 large shallots, finely chopped
2 garlic cloves, minced
1 tablespoon cold-pressed extra virgin olive oil
2 tablespoons butter
1 cup white wine
¼ cup parsley, finely chopped
salt & pepper to taste
1 drop dōTERRA fennel essential oil
1 drop dōTERRA thyme essential oil

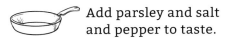 **Add parsley and salt and pepper to taste.**

DIRECTIONS

Add olive oil to a large, deep sauté pan over medium heat. Add shallots and cook 3-5 minutes, stirring occasionally until translucent.

Add butter, garlic, salt, and pepper and stir until garlic becomes aromatic.

Add white wine and turn up the heat to bring the mixture to a simmer. Simmer for 3-5 minutes.

Turn the heat down to medium and add fennel and thyme essential oils, stirring thoroughly.

Add mussels and cover the pot. Cook for 4-5 minutes (until all the shells of the mussels open up).

The "Drop Down" is on the next page.

THE "DROP" DOWN

Fennel essential oil has a sweet, herbaceous aroma with a taste similar to licorice. It's a wonderful digestion aid and can be found in the foods of many cultures that use it for that purpose.

Thyme essential oil has a warm herbaceous and floral aroma. When taken internally, thyme has very potent antioxidant benefits and can support a healthy immune system. During the Middles Ages, there was a belief that it helped instill courage, and it was given to men before they went into battle. It was also used by the ancient Greek and Egyptians for its cleansing and purifying properties.

Indian-Inspired BBQ CHICKEN

MAKES 4-6 SERVINGS

I love finger food, especially when it's tapas style. These are a delicious take on barbecue, but with an Indian flavor flare. Again, a cast-iron skillet is the way to go. The skillet sears the chicken like no other pan does, leaving it crispy on the outside and juicy on the inside.

Also, here's a little bonus: If you like Asian flavors, use the same cooking directions, but replace the sauce with Lemongrass and Ginger Pan-Asian Dressing (page 43), which in this case would be a marinade. If you are a straight-up BBQ person, use Essential Maple-Bourbon BBQ Sauce (page 59). I also encourage you to get creative. There are several dressing and sauce recipes in this book that would work really well here—have fun experimenting!

INGREDIENTS

2 pounds chicken drumsticks (about 8 drumsticks)
½ cup yellow mustard
¼ cup maple syrup
1 tablespoon cold-pressed extra virgin olive oil
½ teaspoon garlic powder
½ teaspoon salt
¼ cup scallions, thinly sliced
2 drops dōTERRA cardamom essential oil
2 drops dōTERRA black pepper essential oil

THE "DROP" DOWN

Cardamom essential oil has a spicy, fruity aroma and is closely related to ginger. It's very flavorful, making it an ideal choice to use in a variety of recipes. When taken internally, it's very supportive of overall gastrointestinal health and also promotes clear breathing and respiratory health.

Black pepper essential oil has a very soothing aroma. It's very high in the chemistry that allows a high level of antioxidant support to the body. It also aids in digestion and supports healthy circulation. Due to its unique spectrum of aromatics, it acts as a wonderful enhancement to many dishes.

DIRECTIONS

Preheat the oven to 425° F.

Place washed and dried drumsticks in a cast-iron skillet and sprinkle them with salt and garlic powder.

Place in the oven and cook for 5-10 minutes, until skin browns.

In a separate bowl, mix mustard, olive oil, maple syrup, and cardamom and black pepper essential oils until thoroughly blended.

Take the skillet out of the oven and pour the sauce mixture
over the chicken, covering it completely.

Place the skillet back into the oven and let cook for another 15 minutes.

Turn the drumsticks over and let them cook for another 15 minutes. (This allows them to cook more evenly.)

 When done, remove chicken from the oven, cover it with scallions, and serve hot.

RUSTIC CHICKEN *and* WILTED SPINACH

MAKES 6-8 SERVINGS

I love the word rustic as it pertains to cooking—it means made in a plain and simple way. Rustic and purist are synonymous for me. When you use a rustic or purist approach, it's about quality of ingredients, not quantity. At one time, people didn't have access to everything they needed on demand, and it impacted the way they cooked. Dishes were made with seasonal and local ingredients. People used what they had access to, and there was a simplicity in this style of cooking.

I feel inspired to give you ideas on how to use recipes more than once by incorporating them into other recipes. Here's another light and easy dish that allows you to use something else you learned to make from this book—Rosemary and Lemon Detox Dressing. As I mentioned, salad dressings and marinades are truly one and the same. It's a way to bring quick and easy flavor to any dish. When you get in the habit of creating your own dressings and marinades, you know exactly what's in them. And if you are using essential oils, you know there's a little something extra to support overall well-being.

INGREDIENTS

2 pounds chicken cutlets
1 pound baby spinach
⅓ cup Rosemary and Lemon Detox Dressing
  (page 45)
½ cup Kalamata olives, sliced or cut into chunks
cold-pressed extra virgin olive oil
salt & pepper to taste

THE "DROP" DOWN

Rosemary essential oil has a herbaceous and energizing aroma that assists with mental clarity. When used internally, it can assist the body's natural detoxification process, calm the nervous system, and aid digestion.

Lemon essential oil has a bright and citrusy aroma that's very energizing and has the ability to elevate one's mood. When taken internally, it aids with cleansing and detoxification and can also support healthy respiratory function.

DIRECTIONS

Preheat the oven to 425° F.

Cut chicken into small chunks.

Place chicken in a large mixing bowl and cover it with Rosemary and Lemon Detox Dressing. Allow to marinade or 20 minutes.

Place the entire contents of the bowl into a large cast-iron skillet. Place the skillet in the oven for approximately 20 minutes, until the chicken is thoroughly cooked.

Remove the skillet from the oven and place it on the stovetop.

Add spinach to the hot skillet and fold it under the chicken, mixing and allowing the warmth to wilt the spinach completely.

Add kalamata olives, salt, and pepper.

 Plate and drizzle with olive oil to finish.

Essential ORANGE BEEF

MAKES 4-6 SERVINGS

This is a true "pandemic" recipe, straight from the quarantine kitchen. When I imagined this dish into reality, I think we were almost a month into sheltering in place, which means I had cooked almost 90 meals in a row in my kitchen for the two of us (at the time I am writing this part of the book, I'm up to almost 300 meals). On this particular night, I was dreaming about orange beef from my favorite Asian eatery in Portland, Maine. I knew we couldn't have it, so, I made it my mission to recreate it. At least, the healthy version of it, since I was in the midst of doing Whole30 and wasn't eating any sugar or fried foods.

I immediately ran into a roadblock—we had no oranges or orange juice. Remember, we were in the throes of being quarantined and didn't have easy access to all the ingredients we usually do. I was determined, so I turned to my essential oil apothecary and grabbed my wild orange. The results were outstanding, and I decided to include the recipe in this book. I do hope that by the time you are reading this I have been able to return to my favorite Asian eatery—more importantly, I hope it's still in business.

INGREDIENTS

2 small beef fillets, about 4-6 oz. each
2 shallots, finely chopped
3 garlic cloves, minced
Sesame oil
¼ cup coconut aminos
1 teaspoon chili-garlic paste
1 teaspoon salt
¼ cup scallions, chopped
6 drops dōTERRA wild orange essential oil
2 tablespoons sesame seeds

THE "DROP" DOWN

Wild orange essential oil has a bright, citrusy aroma and is very emotionally uplifting as well as energizing to the body and mind. When used internally, it's a wonderful support to both the immune system and digestive system and acts as an overall cleansing tonic. It's actually one of my favorite essential oils!

DIRECTIONS

Place four drops of wild orange essential oil in the coconut aminos. Stir and set aside.

Place two drops of wild orange oil on your hands and massage each of the beef fillets. Put fillets on a plate and add a pinch of salt to both sides.

Place a cast-iron skillet over medium heat and coat with sesame oil. Once the oil gets hot, place the fillets in the skillet and let them sear for five minutes on each side. Remove and allow to rest.

Replenish the skillet with sesame oil, add shallots, and sauté for a few minutes.

Slice the fillets very thin. (They will most likely be raw in the middle, but we will be cooking them again.)

Add garlic, chili paste, beef slices, and coconut aminos to skillet and turn the heat to high. Sauté on high for five minutes, allowing the flavors to mesh together. Stir regularly.

Turn the heat down and add scallions. Sauté for two more minutes and turn the heat off. Cover with sesame seeds and a few pinches of salt.

Serve hot.

I'M 10% *Greek* LAMB MEAT BALLS

MAKES 6-8 SERVINGS

If I have already shared this story, I'm about to share it again. Several years ago, Meredith bought me one of those DNA tests for my birthday. I was over the moon (and not surprised) to find out I am ten-percent Greek! I traveled through Greece right after college and stayed with a Greek friend who, at the time, was spending the summer with family. Almost everyone I met assumed I was Greek and tried to convince me that I was. Well, it turns out they were right—ten-percent right. When I found out, I immediately reached out to my friend who has since moved to her homeland and is raising her own family. I said, "I'm so excited, I'm ten-percent Greek!" She responded, "Of course you are!" I guess one can say that Greeks really recognize themselves in others.

I couldn't be more thrilled, and it certainly explains my love for lamb, which I ate quite a bit when visiting that beautiful country. We Greeks, we love our lamb. If you eat meat, even on occasion, lamb is considered by many to be a superfood in moderation. I love this recipe; it's easy to make and easy to share, and it provides an opportunity to use two other recipes from this book to complete it. Opa!

INGREDIENTS

1 pound ground lamb
1 small red onion, very finely chopped
2 garlic cloves, minced
1 egg, beaten
¼ teaspoon salt
¼ teaspoon black pepper
1 drop dōTERRA oregano essential oil
1 drop dōTERRA coriander essential oil

 You can serve these right in the skillet or on your favorite serving plate. Finish by drizzling with Essential Lemon Tahini Sauce or adding a dollop of Zesty Tzatziki with Spearmint.

DIRECTIONS

Preheat the oven to 425° F.

Mix all ingredients together in a large bowl.

Shape the mixture into tablespoon-sized balls and place them on a cast-iron skillet or baking sheet. (I prefer a cast-iron skillet, always.)

Place in the oven and bake for 20 minutes, or until meatballs look crisp and are cooked through the inside.

The "Drop Down" is on the next page.

THE "DROP" DOWN

Oregano essential oil is a wonderful addition to many cuisines around the world. It has a very herbaceous and sharp aroma and is one of the most powerful of all the essential oils. It's so potent that one should practice caution when using it. Only one to two drops is ever necessary. When taken internally, it can support a very healthy immune system response. It's also used as a powerful cleansing and purifying agent.

Coriander essential oil has a wonderful and unique aromatic that's very green and herbaceous with a touch of a floral note. Adding this into any dish helps the body's digestion.

Savory SOUPS

Soups aren't exactly tapas, but they are one of the most caring and nurturing meals we can feed to the people we love. There truly is nothing like a big pot of soup simmering on the stovetop to share with family and friends. Soups heal us and connect us. Why do you think they call it a soup kitchen?

Every culture has their infinite soup recipes. You could host an around-the-world dinner party and have only soups. Hey, that's a great idea!

The last thing I will share about my love for soup is my love for essential oil–infused soup. Soups are one of the easiest meals to infuse with this extra goodness. Talk about aromatic integration! Adding a couple of drops into a hot, steamy broth is like taking a trip to the spa, right in your bowl.

Southeast ASIAN—INSPIRED HAPPY SOUP

MAKES 4-6 SERVINGS

Over the years I picked up a tip or two on how to cook Asian food from some of my Asian friends and, quite frankly, from eating a ton of Asian food. I find Asian foods to be very comforting, especially the soups. I call this happy soup because it makes me smile. I've also called it medicine soup, because I believe happiness is medical.

I love making this for friends. I place all of the toppings in little bowls and cover the table, and it looks like a painting. We all get to choose what and how much of each thing we want in the bowl. It's an interactive meal and makes everyone feel like they are a part of the creation.

Butternut squash soup screams comfort food. Its warm and fuzzy feel makes it a staple wintertime meal in our home. It's wholesome, hearty, creamy, nourishing, and absolutely delicious. This recipe is filled with flavor and will give your immune system a boost while also supporting digestion.

INGREDIENTS

1 large butternut squash
1 garlic bulb
1 box (32 oz) vegetable broth
1 cup almond milk
1 tablespoon cold-pressed extra virgin olive oil
salt & pepper to taste
1 drop dōTERRA ginger essential oil
1 drop dōTERRA clove essential oil
½ cup toasted pepitas for garnish
1 teaspoon smoked paprika for garnish

THE "DROP" DOWN

Ginger essential oil has a spicy, earthy aroma that can be emotionally empowering to individuals feeling stuck. When ingested, it's the perfect digestion aid and can assist with various types of digestive discomfort, including sensitivity to motion while traveling.

Clove essential oil has a very soothing, warm, and spicy aroma. It has very high antioxidant properties and can be a great support to the cardiovascular system as well as enhance immunity.

DIRECTIONS

Preheat the oven to 450° F.

Cut the butternut squash in half and remove the seeds.

Place the squash on a baking sheet, skin down. (You can also choose to take the skin off and cut it into chunks, but this is a much easier approach and works just as well.) Drizzle with olive oil, salt, and pepper.

Take the garlic bulb and remove the outside layer of skin. Cut the head of the garlic off, about ¼-inch from the top, and drizzle the bulb with a little olive oil.

Place the butternut squash and garlic bulb in the oven for about 30 minutes, until the butternut squash is golden brown. Both should be ready at the same time.

Remove from the oven and let cool for 20 minutes.

With a large spoon, scoop the roasted squash out of the skin and into a Vitamix, food processor, or blender. With a small spoon, scoop each garlic clove out of the garlic bulb and add them to the squash.

Add vegetable broth and almond milk. Blend the squash mixture until it reaches the consistency of a creamy bisque.

Return the mix to a stovetop pot and heat on low for 5-10 minutes. Add ginger and clove essential oils and stir until thoroughly blended. Add more salt and pepper to taste.

 Serve in your favorite bowl and garnish with toasted pepitas and a pinch of smoked paprika.

Immune-Boosting TOMATO SPINACH SOUP

MAKES 6 SERVINGS

Seriously, who doesn't love a hot bowl of tomato soup on a cold winter's day? It's a classic that's usually best paired with a grilled cheese sandwich or crusty bread you can dip right into the concoction, making it the quintessential winter lunch.

This recipe doubles down on its elevation factor. Elevation factor number one is the spinach. Tomatoes and spinach are like a savory version of peanut butter and jelly for me; they fit perfectly together. Adding spinach to this soup gives it a nice super-greens punch and legit vegetable credentials. Elevation factor number two is the oregano essential oil. This oil is literally one of the best immune-enhancing oils there is, and the flavor factor, when used correctly, is off the hook.

A bowl of this soup is so healthy that it actually cancels out the grilled cheese or crusty bread if you have it.

INGREDIENTS

1 can (28 oz) crushed tomatoes
1 box (32 oz) vegetable or chicken broth
1 large white onion, finely chopped
2 garlic cloves, minced
1 tablespoon butter
1 tablespoon cold-pressed extra virgin olive oil
½ cup almond milk
2 cups baby spinach leaves
¼ teaspoon salt
¼ teaspoon black pepper
Pinch of crushed red pepper
2 drops dōTERRA oregano essential oil

DIRECTIONS

Heat oil and butter over medium-low heat in a stock pot (I use a Dutch oven). Add onion and garlic and cook, stirring occasionally, until soft.

Add tomatoes, broth, almond milk (feel free to use whole milk or heavy cream if you are feeling decadent), salt, pepper, and a pinch of crushed red pepper.

Bring to a simmer over medium-high heat while stirring. Reduce heat to low, cover, and let simmer for 30 minutes.

Add oregano essential oil (please be mindful to only use two drops—anything more will be too much). Stir thoroughly and then fold in the baby spinach. The heat of the soup should wilt the spinach.

 Serve in your favorite soup bowl with crusty bread or a grilled cheese sandwich. Don't forget to drizzle a little extra olive oil over the top.

THE "DROP" DOWN

Oregano essential oil is a wonderful addition to many cuisines around the world. It has a very herbaceous and sharp aroma and is one of the most powerful of all the essential oils. It's so potent that one should practice caution when using it. Only one to two drops is ever necessary. When taken internally, it can support a very healthy immune system response. It's also used as a powerful cleansing and purifying agent.

I WISH I WAS *Tuscan* BEAN SOUP

MAKES 6 SERVINGS

I am very connected to Italian culture. I grew up outside of Providence, Rhode Island, where there is a large Italian population. Most of my friends were Italian, and they always called me a pizza bagel because I was the Jewish kid who fit in with all of them so well. I've also been to Italy many times; it's a country that truly understands food and the importance of sharing meals with people we love. I have been making and sharing this soup for years. The combination of these oils gives it a particular flavor unique to Tuscany and reminds me of what it smells like there in the spring.

INGREDIENTS

2 cans (15.5 oz) cannellini beans
1 box (32 oz) vegetable or chicken broth
1 large onion, finely chopped
2 celery stalks, finely chopped
3 carrots, chopped
2 garlic cloves, minced
¼ teaspoon salt
¼ teaspoon black pepper
3 tablespoons cold-pressed extra virgin olive oil
1 drop dōTERRA rosemary essential oil
1 drop dōTERRA thyme essential oil
1 drop dōTERRA marjoram essential oil

 Serve in your favorite bowl and drizzle with cold-pressed extra virgin olive oil and cracked black pepper. Shaved Parmesan cheese is a lovely addition if you eat dairy.

DIRECTIONS

Heat olive oil over medium-low heat in a stock pot (I use a Dutch oven).

Add the onions, celery, and garlic and cook, stirring occasionally, until soft.

Drain cannellini beans. (Some people prefer to use dried beans. If this is you, make sure to soak them overnight. You will want about 2 cups of beans. Make sure you cook the beans until they are soft before beginning the soup.)

Add beans, vegetable stock, salt, and pepper to the stock pot. Bring to a simmer over medium- high heat while stirring. Reduce the heat to low, cover, and let simmer for 30 minutes.

Transfer the mix into a Vitamix, food processor, or blender and blend thoroughly until it looks creamy.

Transfer the mixture back into the stock pot. Add carrots and stir thoroughly. Reduce the heat to low, cover, and let simmer for about 10 minutes, until the carrots soften a little.

Add rosemary, thyme, and marjoram essential oils and stir thoroughly.

The "Drop Down" is on the next page.

THE "DROP" DOWN

Rosemary essential oil has a herbaceous and energizing aroma that assists with mental clarity. When used internally, it can assist the body's natural detoxification process, calm the nervous system, and aid digestion.

Thyme essential oil has a warm herbaceous and floral aroma. When taken internally, thyme has very potent antioxidant benefits and can support a healthy immune system. During the Middles Ages, there was a belief that it helped instill courage, and it was given to men before they went into battle. It was also used by the ancient Greek and Egyptians for its cleansing and purifying properties.

Marjoram essential oil has been recognized by ancient cultures as a symbol of happiness. It adds a unique flavor to soups, stews, sauces, dressings, and marinades. It's widely known for its calming effects on the mind and body, especially when used during a massage. When ingested, it may contribute to a healthy cardiovascular system.

Aromatic DAHL

MAKES 6 SERVINGS

Dahl is the Indian culture's term for dishes prepared using lentils, peas, or beans using a certain method. I absolutely love Dahl and think it's a very easy and healthy thing to whip up, especially when you need to feed a lot of people. I lean toward using red lentils for my Dahl because I love the way they taste and because they cook a lot faster due to their tiny size.

INGREDIENTS

1 cup red lentils, rinsed
1 yellow onion, diced
4 garlic cloves, minced
1 sweet potato, peeled and diced
1 tablespoon sesame oil
¼ teaspoon salt
¼ teaspoon pepper
1 drop dōTERRA turmeric essential oil
1 drop dōTERRA ginger essential oil
1 drop dōTERRA cardamom essential oil
½ cup cilantro, chopped, for garnish

DIRECTIONS

Place a large pot over medium heat. Add sesame oil, onions, and garlic and cook until fragrant, stirring occasionally.

Place the rinsed lentils along with 3 cups of water into the same pot. Turn the heat to high and bring to a boil. Once boiling, turn the heat to medium and add sweet potato, salt, and pepper. Cook for 30 minutes.

Turn the heat off and add turmeric, ginger, and cardamom essential oils.

The "Drop Down" is on the next page.

 Garnish with cilantro and serve as a soup or over basmati rice. Adding a slice of naan never hurt anyone, either.

AROMATIC DAHL

THE "DROP" DOWN

Turmeric essential oil has a spicy and earthy aroma. It has been a key botanical in Ayurveda, India's primary health philosophy. The aroma is very grounding and provides a sense of support to individuals when there is a lot of change or uncertainty. Turmeric essential oil has a myriad |of benefits, from providing antioxidant and immune support to supporting healthy glucose and lipid metabolism. It's one of the many essential oils that provides endless benefits to our overall health and wellness when incorporated into a daily routine.

Ginger essential oil has a spicy, earthy aroma that can be emotionally empowering to individuals feeling stuck. When ingested, it's the perfect digestion aid and can assist with various types of digestive discomfort, including sensitivity to motion while traveling.

Cardamom essential oil has a spicy, fruity aroma and is closely related to ginger. It's very flavorful, making it an ideal choice to use in a variety of recipes. When taken internally, it's very supportive of overall gastrointestinal health and also promotes clear breathing and respiratory health.

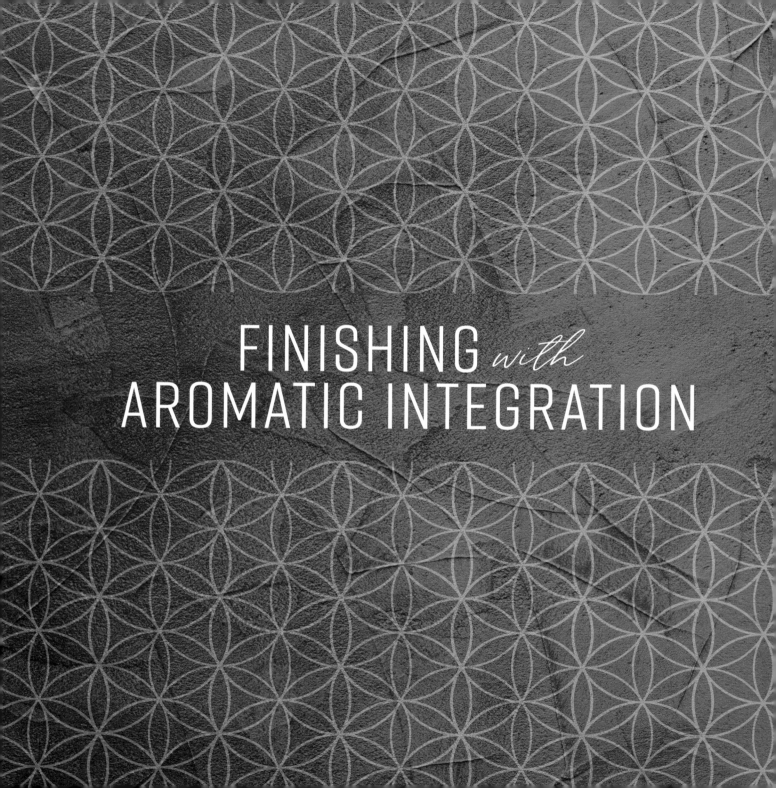

FINISHING *with*
AROMATIC INTEGRATION

In my last book, *The Essential Mixologist,* I introduced the idea of infusing essential oils into cocktails, mocktails, and elixirs. It's a sweet collection of 22 original recipes, laying out a roadmap for the purist perspective and an invitation to play with your inner alchemist using beautiful dōTERRA essential oils. Truth be told, I have enough ideas to create volumes of drink recipes, and I continue to create new ones on a regular basis. Since its release, many people have used *The Essential Mixologist* to enhance their mixology skills and serve up some pretty tasty cocktails—all with health-enhancing properties.

I think it's important to never forget your roots. While *The Essential Foodie* is mainly a food recipe book, I also wanted to offer a continuation of the mixology journey. In this chapter, you will find a collection of 10 non-alcoholic recipes (often referred to as mocktails), as well as some straightforward elixir recipes that can easily be incorporated into your life when you need them. I hope you enjoy these drinks as much as I do, and better yet, I hope you will share them with the people you love. A drink alone can be contemplative, but a drink with a friend adds to that connective tissue and can help you navigate endless hours of good conversation, creating memories that last a lifetime. Cheers!

Essential CHAI

MAKES 8 SERVINGS

Most people love a good cup of chai these days. The spices used in traditional chai are all aromatic and can be found as essential oils. There is a reason why many traditional Indian people drink this on a daily basis as part of a good heath regime. Not only are the spices fragrant and flavorful, but with the addition of these ingredients, the drink becomes an elixir and has the ability to support mood, digestion, blood sugar, and even a healthy respiratory system.

I believe tea, especially chai, is one of those things meant to be shared with others. Since the essential oils used are very potent, this recipe can serve up to eight people. If it's just you, still follow the recipe and save the rest in a Mason jar in the fridge for another time. Simply heat it up on a low flame to warm it and enjoy all over again.

INGREDIENTS

8 black tea bags
1 cup water
4 cups plant-based milk
2-4 tablespoons maple syrup (more if you like it sweeter)
1 drop dōTERRA cinnamon essential oil
1 drop dōTERRA cardamom essential oil
1 drop dōTERRA ginger essential oil
1 drop dōTERRA clove essential oil
1 drop dōTERRA black pepper essential oil

DIRECTIONS

In a saucepan, bring water to a boil. Turn the heat off and let teabags steep for 3-5 minutes.

Remove teabags and discard.

Add plant-based milk, maple syrup, and essential oils. Turn the heat on medium-to-low and whisk the mixture until frothy, then turn the heat off.

 Serve in your favorite mug or glass.

THE "DROP" DOWN

Cinnamon essential oil is a compilation of spicy, woody, warm, and sweet. It has a long history of being used in the culinary world and makes a wonderful addition to many recipes. When ingested, it can support healthy metabolic function and a robust immune system. Since this is a caustic oil, please use it mindfully. Always dilute it with fractionated coconut oil when applying directly to the skin and mindfully inhale when using aromatically.

Cardamom essential oil has a spicy, fruity aroma and is closely related to ginger. It's very flavorful, making it an ideal choice to use in a variety of recipes. When taken internally, it's very supportive of overall gastrointestinal health and also promotes clear breathing and respiratory health.

Ginger essential oil has a spicy, earthy aroma that can be emotionally empowering to individuals feeling stuck. When ingested, it's the perfect digestion aid and can assist with various types of digestive discomfort, including sensitivity to motion while traveling.

Clove essential oil has a very soothing, warm, and spicy aroma. It has very high antioxidant properties and can be a great support to the cardiovascular system as well as enhance immunity.

Black pepper essential oil has a very soothing aroma. It's very high in the chemistry that allows a high level of antioxidant support to the body. It also aids in digestion and supports healthy circulation. Due to its unique spectrum of aromatics, it acts as a wonderful enhancement to many dishes.

Medicinal MOCHA

MAKES 2 SERVINGS

Other than the occasional cup, Meredith and I didn't start drinking coffee until a few years ago. We were in Costa Rica on a trip we won, and Costa Rica is known for its coffee. We were staying at this cool little boutique hotel, and every morning during breakfast they brought us a French press steeping with coffee grown right on their land. I already mentioned that I'm a sucker for farm-to-table stuff, or in this case, plantation to press. We both fell in love with the ritual and decided to take it up in our own home.

Each morning we indulge in one cup of high-quality coffee steeped in a French press, and it's perfect. If you are a coffee drinker, feel free to substitute this recipe with the real thing. It's equally delicious, with all the benefits of coffee. I personally recommend giving the chicory a chance—it's a comparable experience, minus the caffeine. The first time I had chicory was in New Orleans. It was accompanied by a plate of beignets, so the sugar rush may have replaced the missing caffeine—but that's a story for another time.

INGREDIENTS

4 tablespoons roasted chicory root
1 cup almond milk
2 tablespoons raw cacao powder
4 large dates (pits removed)
1 drop dōTERRA cassia essential oil
2 drops dōTERRA wild orange essential oil

DIRECTIONS

If you have a French press, you can steep the chicory the same way you would coffee.

In a separate saucepan, warm the almond milk on the stovetop over low heat.

Add almond milk and the rest of the ingredients to a Vitamix or blender and blend thoroughly.

 Serve in your favorite mug.

THE "DROP" DOWN

Cassia essential oil is very closely related to cinnamon, and interestingly enough, dates back to the Old Testament. Its aromatic is warm and uplifting. When taken internally, it can support healthy digestion and cardiovascular and immune function. Like cinnamon, it also can be caustic and should be diluted with fractionated coconut oil when applied directly to the skin, as well as inhaled mindfully.

Wild orange essential oil has a bright, citrusy aroma and is very emotionally uplifting as well as energizing to the body and mind. When used internally, it's a wonderful support to both the immune system and digestive system and acts as an overall cleansing tonic. It's actually one of my favorite essential oils!

Hot MATCHA LOVE

MAKES 1-2 SERVINGS

There's a drink recipe in *The Essential Mixologist* called "Matcha Love." I love drinking matcha green tea. It has so many wonderful properties that contribute to health and well-being. Adding ginger essential oil makes it an elixir with double the power. The ginger is warming, soothing, and great for digestion. Most importantly, this drink is filled with love.

INGREDIENTS

1 tablespoon matcha
1 cup almond milk
2 tablespoons honey
1 drop dōTERRA ginger essential oil

DIRECTIONS

Put almond milk in a small saucepan and heat on low. Once it's warm, add matcha and gently whisk.

Turn the heat off. In a separate bowl, add ginger essential oil to the honey, mix, and add to the matcha. Continue whisking until it gets a little frothy.

 Serve in your favorite mug and enjoy.

THE "DROP" DOWN

Ginger essential oil has a spicy, earthy aroma that can be emotionally empowering to individuals feeling stuck. When ingested, it's the perfect digestion aid and can assist with various types of digestive discomfort, including sensitivity to motion while traveling. traveling.

Wake-Up CALL IMMUNE BOOSTER

MAKES 2 SERVINGS

You know those days when you wake up and something feels off in your body? Maybe your throat feels scratchy, your energy is low, and you feel like your immune system needs a little extra support. Well, help is on the way. This is the perfect elixir to get you back on track.

INGREDIENTS

2 cups baby spinach leaves
½ cup coconut water
2 lemons, squeezed for juice
1 tablespoon raw honey
¼ teaspoon cayenne pepper
1 drop dōTERRA On Guard® essential oil

DIRECTIONS

Place all ingredients in a Vitamix or blender and blend for 30 seconds.

 Serve in a glass and drink it down—it's got a little kick, so you might want a water chaser.

THE "DROP" DOWN

On Guard® essential oil is a proprietary essential oil blend that provides a natural and effective alternative for immune support when used internally. As one of dōTERRA's best-selling blends, dōTERRA On Guard protects against environmental and seasonal threats with essential oils known for their positive effects on the immune system when ingested. dōTERRA On Guard can be taken internally on a daily basis to maintain healthy immune function and support healthy cardiovascular function. It can also be used on surfaces throughout the home as a non-toxic cleaner. When diffused, dōTERRA On Guard helps purify the air and can be very energizing and uplifting.

Photo courtesy of Julez Weinberg

Morning FOG LIFTER

MAKES 1 SERVING

If you ever have a night where you had more than you should have—whether it's that extra glass of wine, one too many beers, or a few too many cocktails—this elixir is a lifeline back to health. The secret is the rosemary and lemon essential oil combination: it helps the body metabolize alcohol. Here's the deal, though—now that you know this little secret, don't use it as an excuse to go nuts all the time. Every now and then it happens to the best of us, and now you have some help when you need it. Pass it on!

INGREDIENTS

1 cup coconut water
1 drop dōTERRA rosemary essential oil
1 drop dōTERRA lemon essential oil

 Combine all ingredients in a Mason jar and shake. Add ice if desired and drink it down.

THE "DROP" DOWN

Rosemary essential oil has a herbaceous and energizing aroma that assists with mental clarity. When used internally, it can assist the body's natural detoxification process, calm the nervous system, and aid digestion.

Lemon essential oil has a bright and citrusy aroma that's very energizing and has the ability to elevate one's mood. When taken internally, it aids with cleansing and detoxification and can also support healthy respiratory function.

Tummy TAMER

MAKES 1 SERVING

In Italy, they always end a meal with a *digestivo*, a drink made by infusing brandy with a variety of herbs; aromatic roots and bark; spices; citrus peels; and flowers. If you have ever eaten a meal in Italy, they usually consist of at least four courses and last several hours. The tradition of sipping a digestivo after meals is social, but also offers digestive support—something most can use after an Italian meal.

I would call this recipe an alcohol-free digestivo hack. It's not the work of a genius alchemist; I'm just using one of our top essential oil blends when it comes to aiding with digestion and doing a couple of simple things to make it an enjoyable beverage to share with friends after a meal.

INGREDIENTS

1 cup carbonated "fizzy" water
1 teaspoon raw honey
1 drop dōTERRA DigestZen® essential oil
orange rind or shaved orange
   peel for garnish

DIRECTIONS

Add DigestZen essential oil to the honey and mix. Add the honey mixture to the fizzy water and gently mix.

 Serve over a few ice cubes and garnish with orange rind or shaved orange peel—this adds a bitter element for flavor contrast and makes the drink pretty enough to serve to guests.

THE "DROP" DOWN

DigestZen® essential oil is well known for its ability to aid in digestion, soothe occasional stomach upset, and maintain overall digestive health when taken internally. This unique blend contains ginger, fennel, and coriander to help ease occasional stomach discomfort, including motion sickness and indigestion, while peppermint, tarragon, anise, and caraway aid with digestion and help maintain a healthy gastrointestinal tract.

CUCUMBER *Cooler*

MAKES 2 SERVINGS

Sometimes we want a festive drink without the addition of alcohol, and this one knocks it out of the park every time. It's delicious on its own, and if you feel like you need a little something extra, add two ounces of your favorite spirit to this drink: tequila, rum, whisky, vodka, gin—they all work well here.

Please don't be intimidated by the cucumber juice. It's easy to make and very healthy for you. It stores well in a Mason jar and can keep for several days. Once you use it to make a Cucumber Cooler, those leftovers can also be stored in the same way and will keep a little longer with the addition of the essential oils, which act as a preservative.

CUCUMBER JUICE INGREDIENTS

1 medium-sized cucumber, peeled and cut
  into chunks
2 cups water

DIRECTIONS

Place cucumber in Vitamix or blender.

Add water and blend.

 Transfer to a Mason jar, cover tightly, and store in the refrigerator.

CUCUMBER COOLER INGREDIENTS

10 oz cucumber juice
1 lime, squeezed for juice
2 tablespoons maple syrup
1 drop dōTERRA spearmint essential oil
2 drops dōTERRA tangerine essential oil
fizzy water
mint spring or cucumber peel for garnish

DIRECTIONS

Add maple syrup to a pitcher. Add spearmint and tangerine essential oils to the maple syrup and mix them together.

Add cucumber juice and squeeze lime into the mixture. Mix thoroughly.

 Serve in an 8-to-10-ounce glass over ice, finished off with 2 ounces of fizzy water.

Garnish with a mint sprig or cucumber peel.

CUCUMBER COOLER

THE "DROP" DOWN

Spearmint essential oil has a refreshing, sweet aroma that's very emotionally uplifting. When taken internally, it can aid in digestion and assist with an upset stomach.

Tangerine essential oil has a sweet and tangy aroma. It's known for its ability to energize and uplift one's mood. When used internally, it can support the immune system and act as a cleansing and purifying tonic to the body.

Gin-less JUNIPER SPRITZ

MAKES 1 SERVING

Did you know that gin is made from juniper berries, along with an array of other interesting botanicals? In my book, *The Essential Mixologist*, I provide a beautiful recipe for lavender lemonade paired with a gin cocktail. It's a truly enchanting cocktail, but if you don't consume alcohol, you miss the magic of the juniper berry. Well, I couldn't have this happen on my watch, so I got to work. The results are the Gin-less Juniper Spritz. I hope you enjoy playing with the juniper berry; she's a special botanical.

HOMEMADE LEMONADE INGREDIENTS

10 cups spring water
1 cup raw honey
8 lemons, squeezed for juice

DIRECTIONS

Warm 10 cups of spring water with honey until the honey dissolves, and then let the mixture cool.

Add the juice of 8 lemons, stir thoroughly, and distribute into 16-ounce glass bottles.

Cover tightly and store in the refrigerator for later use.

GIN-LESS JUNIPER SPRITZ INGREDIENTS

4 oz Homemade Lemonade
1 drop dōTERRA juniper berry essential oil
carbonated "fizzy" water
lemon shavings for garnish

DIRECTIONS

Place ice in a shaker. Add Homemade Lemonade and juniper berry essential oil. Cover tightly and shake.

 Fill an 8-ounce glass with ice and pour the contents of the shaker over the ice. Fill the rest of the glass with fizzy water (about 4 ounces).

Garnish with lemon shavings and enjoy!

THE "DROP" DOWN

Juniper berry essential oil has a very calming and grounding aromatic. It's used in a variety of culinary cuisines and is one of the primary botanicals in gin. When consumed, it supports healthy kidney and urinary tract function.

Indian-Spiced SPRITZ

MAKES 1 SERVING

If you haven't yet noticed, I have a small affinity for Indian flavors, with their array of exotic spices. I find the aromatics used in this cuisine emotionally uplifting and very supportive to my physical well-being, especially when it comes to digestion. This drink is a perfect mocktail, but if you find yourself wanting to spike it with a spirit, vodka, whiskey, rum, or even tequila would make a fine choice.

INGREDIENTS

4 oz ginger beer
½ lime, squeezed for juice
1 drop dōTERRA cardamom essential oil
fizzy water
edible flower for garnish

DIRECTIONS

 Place ginger beer in an 8-ounce glass. Squeeze in lime, add cardamom essential oil, and stir thoroughly.

Add ice and fill the rest of the glass with fizzy water. Give it a light stir.

Garnish with edible flower and enjoy!

THE "DROP" DOWN

Cardamom essential oil has a spicy, fruity aroma and is closely related to ginger. It's very flavorful, making it an ideal choice to use in a variety of recipes. When taken internally, it's very supportive of overall gastrointestinal health and also promotes clear breathing and respiratory health.

Vegan EGGLESS NOG

MAKES 4-6 SERVINGS

Every holiday season is the same for me. I go to a holiday party, and someone offers me an eggnog. At the time, it sounds like a good idea —a joyful and festive beverage full of holiday cheer! Two sips in and I remember, once again, that I hate eggnog. Spiced liquid chicken, yuck!

One year I thought to myself, how does it get any better than this? What else is possible with eggnog? It's a fine and delightful idea. What would it take for me to actually like it enough to drink it? Vegan Eggless Nog was the result of that question. If you like to spike your eggnog, adding two ounces of brandy, rum, or whisky will make you feel holly and jolly.

INGREDIENTS

1 can (15.5 oz) organic coconut milk
½ cup raw cashews
6 pitted dates
¼ cup cold water
1 teaspoon vanilla
2 drops dōTERRA clove essential oil
2 drops dōTERRA cinnamon essential oil
2 drops dōTERRA ginger essential oil
cinnamon or nutmeg for garnish

DIRECTIONS

Combine all ingredients in a blender or Vita Mix until completely blended.

 Serve straight up in a glass, or over ice.

Garnish with a pinch of cinnamon or nutmeg.

THE "DROP" DOWN

Clove essential oil has a very soothing, warm, and spicy aroma. It has very high antioxidant properties and can be a great support to the cardiovascular system as well as enhance immunity.

Cinnamon essential oil is a compilation of spicy, woody, warm, and sweet. It has a long history of being used in the culinary world and makes a wonderful addition to many recipes. When ingested, it can support healthy metabolic function and a robust immune system. Since this is a caustic oil, please use it mindfully. Always dilute it with fractionated coconut oil when applying directly to the skin and mindfully inhale when using aromatically.

Ginger essential oil has a spicy, earthy aroma that can be emotionally empowering to individuals feeling stuck. When ingested, it's the perfect digestion aid and can assist with various types of digestive discomfort, including sensitivity to motion while traveling.

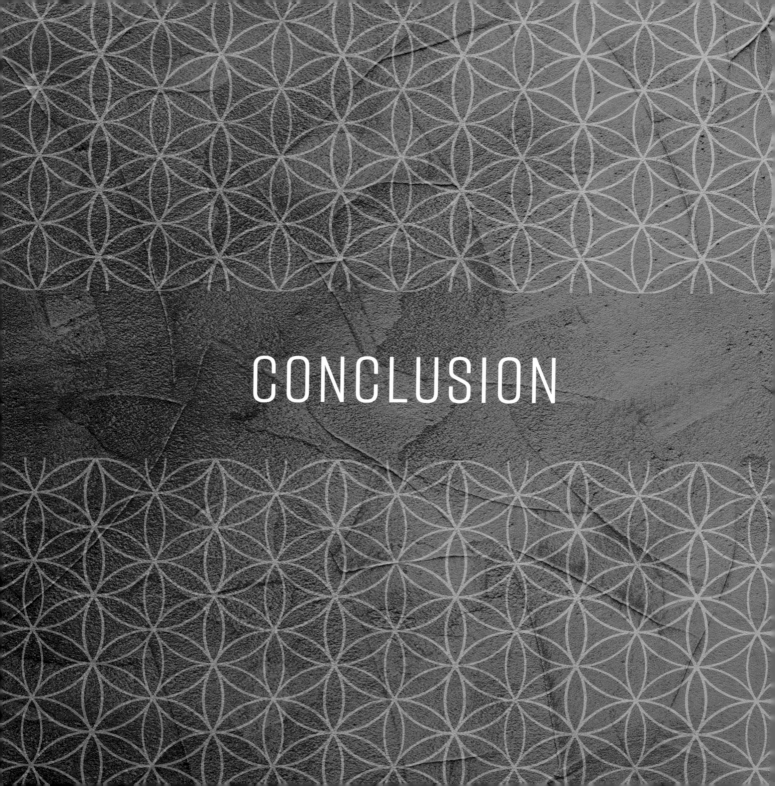

CONCLUSION

The ESSENTIAL FOODIE KIT

Basil	Clove	Lavender	Pink pepper
Black pepper	Coriander	Lemon	Rosemary
Cardamom	DigestZen®	Lemongrass	Spearmint
Cassia	Fennel	Lime	Tangerine
Cilantro	Ginger	Marjoram	Thyme
Cinnamon	Grapefruit	On Guard®	Turmeric
Clary sage	Juniper berry	Oregano	Wild orange

dōTERRA® is a wonderful choice for all of your essential oil needs. They also carry many other essential oil–enhanced wellness products. If you don't already have a dōTERRA account, please feel free to contact me and we will set you up with a wholesale account, giving you access to very deep discounts on these incredible products. If someone has been speaking with you already about dōTERRA, please honor that relationship and contact them for guidance on getting started.

There is also an incredible business opportunity for those who are passionate about health and wellness and enjoy helping others. We are always looking for new people to join our team and would be happy to connect with anyone who is genuinely interested in our business.

For more information, please visit www.cultivate-wellness.com.

THE DROP DOWN *Index*

Basil essential oil has a very herbaceous and refreshing aroma. It is a wonderful support to the body regarding inflammation and has an energizing and restorative quality.

Black pepper essential oil has a very soothing aroma. It's very high in the chemistry that allows a high level of antioxidant support to the body. It also aids in digestion and supports healthy circulation. Due to its unique spectrum of aromatics, it acts as a wonderful enhancement to many dishes.

Cardamom essential oil has a spicy, fruity aroma and is closely related to ginger. It's very flavorful, making it an ideal choice to use in a variety of recipes. When taken internally, it's very supportive of overall gastrointestinal health and also promotes clear breathing and respiratory health.

Cassia essential oil is very closely related to cinnamon, and interestingly enough, dates back to the Old Testament. Its aromatic is warm and uplifting. When taken internally, it can support healthy digestion and cardiovascular and immune function. Like cinnamon, it also can be caustic and should be diluted with fractionated coconut oil when applied directly to the skin, as well as inhaled mindfully.

Cilantro essential oil has a very fresh, bright, and herbal aromatic. When used internally, it promotes healthy digestion, supports a good immune system response, and nourishes the nervous system. Cilantro is also known for its ability to aid the body's detox response to heavy metals through chelation.

Cinnamon essential oil is a compilation of spicy, woody, warm, and sweet. It has a long history of being used in the culinary world and makes a wonderful addition to many recipes. When ingested, it can support healthy metabolic function and a robust immune system. Since this is a caustic oil, please use it mindfully. Always dilute it with fractionated coconut oil when applying directly to the skin and mindfully inhale when using aromatically.

Clary sage essential oil has a woody, herbal aroma. When taken internally as well as used aromatically, it has a very calming effect on the psyche, promotes relaxation, and can contribute to a restful night's sleep.

Clove essential oil has a very soothing, warm, and spicy aroma. It has very high antioxidant properties and can be a great support to the cardiovascular system as well as enhance immunity.

Coriander essential oil has a wonderful and unique aromatic that's very green and herbaceous with a touch of a floral note. Adding this into any dish helps the body's digestion.

DigestZen® essential oil is well known for its ability to aid in digestion, soothe occasional stomach upset, and maintain overall digestive health when taken internally. This unique blend contains ginger, fennel, and coriander to help ease occasional stomach discomfort, including motion sickness and indigestion, while peppermint, tarragon, anise, and caraway aid with digestion and help maintain a healthy gastrointestinal tract.

Fennel essential oil has a sweet, herbaceous aroma with a taste similar to licorice. It's a wonderful digestion aid and can be found in the foods of many cultures that use it for that purpose.

Ginger essential oil has a spicy, earthy aroma that can be emotionally empowering to individuals feeling stuck. When ingested, it's the perfect digestion aid and can assist with various types of digestive discomfort, including sensitivity to motion while traveling.

Grapefruit essential oil has a bright and energizing aroma. It can be very uplifting and help increase motivation. When taken internally, it supports a healthy metabolism and helps the body release cellulite in stubborn areas.

Juniper berry essential oil has a very calming and grounding aromatic. It's used in a variety of culinary cuisines and is one of the primary botanicals in gin. When consumed, it supports healthy kidney and urinary tract function.

Lavender essential oil has a light and floral aroma that's very calming to the nervous system. It can be used both aromatically and topically, but when used internally, it can reduce anxious feelings and ease feelings of tension. It can also promote a peaceful night's sleep.

Lemon essential oil has a bright and citrusy aroma that's very energizing and has the ability to elevate one's mood. When taken internally, it aids with cleansing and detoxification and can also support healthy respiratory function.

Lemongrass essential oil has a herbaceous, citrus aroma that can be emotionally uplifting while also inspiring a positive outlook on life. When ingested, it promotes healthy digestion and acts as an overall tonic to the entire body.

Lime essential oil has an uplifting and energizing aroma and adds a bright, citrusy flavor to food. Its purifying qualities make it a wonderful support to the body's internal cleansing process. When taken internally, it provides support to the immune system.

Marjoram essential oil has been recognized by ancient cultures as a symbol of happiness. It adds a unique flavor to soups, stews, sauces, dressings, and marinades. It's widely known for its calming effects on the mind and body, especially when used during a massage. When ingested, it may contribute to a healthy cardiovascular system.

On Guard® essential oil is a proprietary essential oil blend that provides a natural and effective alternative for immune support when used internally. As one of dōTERRA's best-selling blends, dōTERRA On Guard protects against environmental and seasonal threats with essential oils known for their positive effects on the immune system when ingested. dōTERRA On Guard can be taken internally on a daily basis to maintain healthy immune function and support healthy cardiovascular function. It can also be used on surfaces throughout the home as a non-toxic cleaner. When diffused, dōTERRA On Guard® helps purify the air and can be very energizing and uplifting.

Oregano essential oil is a wonderful addition to many cuisines around the world. It has a very herbaceous and sharp aroma and is one of the most powerful of all the essential oils. It's so potent that one should practice caution when using it. Only one to two drops is ever necessary. When taken internally, it can support a very healthy immune system response. It's also used as a powerful cleansing and purifying agent.

THE DROP DOWN INDEX

Pink pepper essential oil has a slightly spicy and fruity aroma. Taking this oil internally supports the immune system and digestive system and helps the body maintain healthy cellular function.

Rosemary essential oil has a herbaceous and energizing aroma that assists with mental clarity. When used internally, it can assist the body's natural detoxification process, calm the nervous system, and aid digestion.

Spearmint essential oil has a refreshing, sweet aroma that's very emotionally uplifting. When taken internally, it can aid in digestion and assist with an upset stomach.

Tangerine essential oil has a sweet and tangy aroma. It's known for its ability to energize and uplift one's mood. When used internally, it can support the immune system and act as a cleansing and purifying tonic to the body.

Thyme essential oil has a warm herbaceous and floral aroma. When taken internally, thyme has very potent antioxidant benefits and can support a healthy immune system. During the Middles Ages, there was a belief that it helped instill courage, and it was given to men before they went into battle. It was also used by the ancient Greek and Egyptians for its cleansing and purifying properties.

Turmeric essential oil has a spicy and earthy aroma. It has been a key botanical in Ayurveda, India's primary health philosophy. The aroma is very grounding and provides a sense of support to individuals when there is a lot of change or uncertainty. Turmeric essential oil has a myriad of benefits, from providing antioxidant and immune support to supporting healthy glucose and lipid metabolism. It's one of the many essential oils that provides endless benefits to our overall health and wellness when incorporated into a daily routine.

Wild orange essential oil has a bright, citrusy aroma and is very emotionally uplifting as well as energizing to the body and mind. When used internally, it's a wonderful support to both the immune system and digestive system and acts as an overall cleansing tonic. It's actually one of my favorite essential oils!

ABOUT *the* AUTHOR

Julez Weinberg has been involved in the world of alchemy since the early nineties and has been working with essential oils since 1999. She is a passionate advocate of whole foods, pure ingredients, and returning to nature for solutions regarding health and wellness. Her extensive background in essential oils and herbs, combined with a health coaching certification from the Institute of Integrative Nutrition, provides her with a wellspring of knowledge to share about nutrition and living a natural lifestyle. She is also a hobby chef, gardener, writer, photographer/filmmaker, and all-around creative being.

Julez currently resides in Kennebunk, Maine, with her spouse and business partner, Meredith, and their adorable Australian labradoodle, Byron. Julez and Meredith have built a very successful business with dōTERRA® and continue to grow their teams globally. *The Essential Foodie* is a follow-up to Julez's first book, *The Essential Mixologist*. It is the second title in an ongoing series of books where she will be sharing her wisdom and love of combining essential oils with food and drink.